PRAISE FOR *FRAMI...*

D0378383

As I write this endorsement for my friend Matt, I a...
my blog, and reading a magazine article. A book about being present to God: ies,
please.

—Jon Acuff, *New York Times* Best-selling Author
of *Start* and *Stuff Christians Like*

Living out our faith in today's distracted and disrupted world is far more difficult
and challenging than most people think. That's why Matt Knisely's fascinating book
Framing Faith is the road map we've been waiting to find. If you're serious about
hearing God through the noise of our digital culture, then this is the book for you.
Order it today, and start cutting through the clutter.

—Phil Cooke, Filmmaker, Media Consultant, and Author of *Unique:
Telling Your Story in the Age of Brands and Social Media*

The creative insight and perspective in this book will help you learn to view life
beyond the typical day-to-day grind and open your eyes so you're wide-awake to see
the extraordinary moments that are all around you.

—Pete Wilson, Senior Pastor, Cross Point Church,
Author of *Plan B* and *Let Hope In*

Framing Faith is an invitation to capture and embrace life's unfolding stories and
moments that ultimately shape our souls. Matt gifts us with new perspectives and
insights into proactively embracing the beauty of life that we far too often take for
granted. Slow down and read this book.

—Charles Lee, CEO of Ideation and Author of *Good Idea. Now What?*

Great photography is about transforming ordinary places and people into extraordinary ones. This book by a great photographer takes that principle and through godly
wisdom applies it to everyday life. To see your life as Matt sees it is to be changed by
God for good.

—The Reverend Canon J. John, www.philotrust.com

Matt Knisely's greatest gift is to frame and capture the beauty of Jesus for our generation and those to come.

—Esther Havens, Humanitarian Photographer

Capturing the perfect moment is magical. In *Framing Faith* Matt captures the perfection of art and faith and makes them accessible for everyone. Every creative believer
needs the lens Matt provides in this book.

—Stephen Brewster, Creative Arts Pastor,
Cross Point Community Church

In a distracted world, this book is urgently needed. Matt puts words to my feeling and shines a light on the clutter that's piled up in my soul. Thanks Matt for making me hungry for more of God and less of this world.

—SCOTT WILSON, SENIOR PASTOR OF THE OAKS
FELLOWSHIP AND AUTHOR OF *READY, SET, GROW*

Matt is an artist with an unbelievable lens to capture what really matters. *Framing Faith* is a long lost prayer for our current distracted culture and reads as if you're having a conversation with a dear friend. The words Matt weaves take root, grow slowly, change our perspective, and point us into a deeper relationship with the Father. As someone who struggles with the anxiety of being overwhelmed, Matt's words were of great comfort and hope.

—ANNE MARIE MILLER, AUTHOR AND SPEAKER, ANNEMARIEMILLER.COM

This book is more than it seems. Like a good photograph, the more you look at it, the more you find. Matt has captured the beauty, and complexity, of life and faith—and given us the tools to navigate them both.

—JEFF GOINS, AUTHOR OF *THE IN-BETWEEN*

I wanted to dog-ear every page in Matt Knisely's *Framing Faith*. It's a narrative about how to tell one's story—yet more than that. It's about how to live to the hilt. Knisely refers to "Chasing Sunsets"—a term he uses to describe those times when passion collides with life. Reading this book was like chasing sunsets for me—my passion collided with life as I soaked in Knisely's masterful words. *Framing Faith* is a shining thread in the tapestry of literature.

—EMILY T. WIERENGA, AUTHOR OF *ATLAS GIRL*, WWW.EMILYWIERENGA.COM

In *Framing Faith* Matt Knisely calls us to an undistracted, honest look at the important themes God is writing into our life stories. This unique and creative book teaches us to slow down, capture the beauty in every moment, and open our eyes to see God working all around us. It is sure to shift paradigms and change the way you see the world.

—KEN WYTSMA, PRESIDENT OF KILNS COLLEGE, LEAD PASTOR
OF ANTIOCH CHURCH, AND AUTHOR OF *PURSUING JUSTICE*

I've always thought of photography as capturing light as a memory so as to never forget. What Matt has compiled here are decades full of light that will shine into all the work you make. May we never forget the lessons that Matt has shared.

—BLAINE HOGAN, CREATIVE DIRECTOR AND AUTHOR OF
UNTITLED: THOUGHTS ON THE CREATIVE PROCESS

From the start of Matt's gripping book, *Framing Faith*, I've had a deep stirring in my heart to refocus on what is truly important. I'm INSPIRED to put my phone down, hug my wife and son, and live a story worth writing about.

—DAVID MOLNAR, MUSIC AND ADVERTISING PHOTOGRAPHER
AND AUTHOR OF *IPHONE ONLY PHOTOGRAPHY*

Are you tired, distracted, over-connected or burned out? Do you feel like your life lacks beauty? You won't want to miss this: the stories, the images, the experience that is curated inside this book. Matt helps us to go deeper, to pay attention, to discover the beauty, meaning and purpose that lies beneath the surface of our lives. Go ahead. I dare you. Dive in.

—ALLISON VESTERFELT, AUTHOR OF *PACKING LIGHT:*
THOUGHTS ON LIVING LIFE WITH LESS BAGGAGE

We all need to have a personal relationship with the Lord. *Framing Faith* guides us back to the foundation we were meant to live from—the place of intimate fellowship with the living God, drawing our identity from Him, our joy from Him, our sense of fulfillment from Him. Matt Knisely delivers concise, godly truth that will cut through and help you develop a deeper, loving relationship with God.

—JONATHAN MORRIS, FOX NEWS CONTRIBUTOR
AND AUTHOR OF *GOD WANTS YOU HAPPY*

Matt Knisely's book, *Framing Faith*, is just further proof that the world—and the church—desperately needs artists. Artists who invite us to go beyond the typical black and white, linear, and comfortable ways of viewing our lives and the world we live in. Bravo to Matt Knisely for giving us a more artful way of recognizing and embracing goodness, beauty, truth, and faith.

—SCOTT HODGE, ARTIST, WANDERER, AND PASTOR
OF THE ORCHARD COMMUNITY

Framing Faith is a book that encourages you to stop, breathe, and truly digest the moments of beauty God ordains within our lives. Matt encourages one to view faith through an entirely new lens.

—JARRID WILSON, PASTOR, BLOGGER, AND AUTHOR OF *JESUS SWAGGER*

Shaw's prophecy was right—art and artists will save the church. Matt is a pirate-captain of this new charge, capturing the heart of a visual generation with the irresistible beauty of the one called Love.

—DR. JOHN SOWERS, PRESIDENT OF THE MENTORING
PROJECT AND AUTHOR OF *THE HEROIC PATH*

Today's bookshelves and websites are filled with books on "story" from writers, thinkers, and pastors. But Matt Knisely, as a photojournalist and storyteller, offers us a thoroughly unique and compelling reflection on how we might better see the truth and beauty God has and is still creating in our lives.

—JOHN DYER, COMMUNICATIONS DIRECTOR, DALLAS THEOLOGICAL
SEMINARY, AND AUTHOR OF *FROM THE GARDEN TO THE CITY*

In our world where unlimited information has become a mere distraction and social media often stands in for real socializing, *Framing Faith* shows us how to live out truly important, meaningful stories with God—stories that cannot be compressed into 140 characters.

—MATT APPLING, EDUCATOR, PASTOR, AUTHOR OF *LIFE AFTER ART*

Framing Faith causes me to think about my own story and to make changes in my life that will create a better ending.

—TRACEY MITCHELL, TV HOST AND AUTHOR OF *DOWNSIDE UP*

If a photo is worth a thousand words, then *Framing Faith* is worth its weight in wisdom only found through true life experiences. This book is not only a challenge for us now, but a good reminder not to lose sight of God's love all around us our entire lives.

—KYLE STEED, PROFESSIONAL DOODLER

Matt has done with words what he does with his camera: he captures a beautiful image that tells a powerful story. Through this verbal imagery, *Framing Faith* provides us with a language for describing the rising art of visual storytelling.

—STEPHEN PROCTOR, VISUAL LITURGIST AND AUTHOR

From the opening pages of *Framing Faith* I found myself saying out loud an emphatic "yes" over and over again. Matt has a unique voice and a wonderful gift of bringing to life our everyday experiences, but reframing them in a profound way. I'm most thankful that the book was a constant example of the importance of slowing down and being mindful of our every moment. For when we are mindful in the moment, we are most aware of God at work in our lives and the transformation that He brings. Thank you, Matt, for continually reminding me of that at each turn of the page.

—RHETT SMITH, MARRIAGE AND FAMILY THERAPIST AND AUTHOR
OF *THE ANXIOUS CHRISTIAN* AND *WHAT IT MEANS TO BE A MAN*

FRAMING FAITH

MATT KNISELY

W PUBLISHING GROUP

AN IMPRINT OF THOMAS NELSON

Published in Nashville, Tennessee, by Thomas Nelson. Thomas Nelson is a registered trademark of Thomas Nelson, Inc.

Published in association with literary agent Blair Jacobson of D.C. Jacobson & Associates, LLC, an Author Management Company, www.dcjacobson.com.

Thomas Nelson, Inc., titles may be purchased in bulk for educational, business, fund-raising, or sales promotional use. For information, please e-mail SpecialMarkets@ ThomasNelson.com.

In some instances, the names of individuals in anecdotes have been changed.

The bulk of the photography used in this book reflects casual in-the-moment photography of life created for this project. To see more of Matt's professional work go to mattknisely.com.

ISBN: 978-0-8499-2187-2

Library of Congress Cataloging-in-Publication Data

Knisely, Matt.
Framing faith / by Matt Knisely.
pages cm
Includes bibliographical references.
ISBN 978-0-8499-2187-2 (trade paper)
1. Christian life. 2. Christianity and art. 3. Spiritual life--Christianity. I. Title.
BV4509.5.K57 2014
248.4--dc23
2013031947

To Starfish, No No, Lou, and my entire family for changing the way I see. And to those who will discover that hope looks forward and faith takes steps into the future.

The greatest moments in life are the ones which we are present for.

CONTENTS

PART 1: FOCUS

Knowing who you are and what you stand for is the foundation of our journey. That understanding gives us the opportunity and freedom to steer and renew the things we'd like to change about ourselves. Without knowing who we are, self-acceptance and change become impossible; our stories matter.

We live in an information-overload age of quick sound bites, 140-characters-or-less communications, status updates, world news in sixty seconds, hashtags, and text messages with ridiculous abbreviations . . . SMH! Our attention span has evaporated. It's as if our culture is against us going too deep or understanding anything at

Contents

a profound level. But if we don't know how to go deep, then we will never be able to truly know ourselves and other people. This has serious implications for our ability to know God.

In a culture of connectivity, we've tuned out personal contact and replaced it with virtual communication. This has left us lonely—oblivious to our environment and effect on others. Story is the shortest distance between two people and ultimately is at the very heart of relationship. From the beginning of time, God intended people to enjoy companionship. He did not intend for us to be lonely, isolated, and switched off from one another.

We find ourselves constantly in "aesthetic arrest" as we live in a perfectionistic culture. We try to achieve beauty in everything we do. Yet the human experience is not perfect: it's flawed. God shows us how beauty comes by way of imperfection through the stories of Sarah, David, Moses, and ultimately what landed Christ on the cross.

In a sea of distractions it's hard to hear God's voice. Yet nothing is more personal or intimate than listening. As we become better listeners, we can not only relate to others but recognize God's voice. When we find ourselves in a spiritual crisis, we can listen to hear God speaking to us amid the din of our lives and against our modern ways of knowing and controlling.

PART 2: CAPTURE

Our lives are filled with milestones, but have we learned to identify the decisive moments God has given us? And are we pinpointing the extraordinary in the "ordinary" moments? Similar to how a photographer sits and waits for the right moment to capture an image, God wants us to be still and learn to recognize these decisive moments with him. To wait in solace. To wait in faith. To wait with hope. To wait in prayer. All so that we may have a moment of understanding.

Like storytellers, God wants us to look for more and develop perspective. He wants us to connect the seemingly unconnected, find what has been overlooked, and worry less about what we do and more about who we can become. God wants to turn our lives upside down and to use us in magnificent, unpredictable, world-changing ways. God's perspective is that we find his will for us and uncover the meaning in the story he has written.

Photographs have one element that never changes: a leading subject. This subject adds meaning and context to the image. The whole photograph centers on this subject and the story that it creates. By design, the Bible shows how God developed central characters to expand his kingdom, and he is forming our lives in the same way.

CONTENTS

CONTENTS

*and we can be different, visible, and engaging. As we
allow God's light to shine through our story, we will see
God at work in our lives and moving in our own hearts.*

FOREWORD

A close friend of mine is an artist of wood and words. He doubles as an Episcopal priest. In 1988, Michael Blewett graduated from Westminster Choir College of Rider University, where my brother John's wife, Sharon Sweet, is on the faculty. The commencement speaker that year happened to be the great choral conductor Robert Shaw (1916–1999). Shaw framed his remarks by showing how, in the premodern, medieval world, it was the church that saved the arts. He challenged the graduates to reverse roles. In the future, he prophesied, artists and the arts would save the church.

Up until now, the church has not been all that hospitable to being rescued by artists and the arts. There has been little revival of the tradition of artistic sponsorship by the church in the form of commissioning of arts or patronage of artists. Willem de Kooning is one of the few artists who can boast finding a home in the church. His glowing, lyrical triptych beams its beauty behind the altar at St. Peter's Lutheran Church in New York City. Three twentieth-century artists in particular—Richard Meier (architect), Frank Stella (painter), and Mies van der Rohe (architect)—decried the fact that they didn't get more commissions from churches. In a 1968 documentary film produced by his daughter Georgia, Mies van der Rohe, age eighty-two, was asked what he most wanted to build that he had not yet built. "A cathedral" was his reply.[1]

Framing Faith by world-class artist Matt Knisely is a glass-case exhibit of the church's increasing openness to those who struggle to create and comprehend beauty. This is coming to pass for a couple of reasons.

First, scientists have begun to think more like artists, and some of their books (see superstring physicist Brian Greene's *The Elegant Universe*[2]) sound at places like they were written by poets. German philosopher Martin Heidegger once observed that the word *technology* is etymologically linked with art rather than science.[3]

Second, theologians and thinkers are rediscovering beauty as "God's most neglected attribute," as Hans Urs von Balthasar put it.[4] God is not only beautiful—God is beauty itself and the source of all beauty, truth, and goodness. Brian Zahnd has taken Dostoevsky's saying in *The Idiot*[5] and turned it into a manifesto called *Beauty Will Save the World*.[6]

Third, in a world where the primary cultural currency is image, not word, the ultimate apologetics is aesthetics. In violinist Yehudi Menuhin's autobiography *Unfinished Journey*, there is a revealing story of how, after one of his concerts, an elderly and frail Albert Einstein clambered slowly over the footlights and embraced Menuhin. Then he shouted to everyone who could hear, "Now I *know* there is a God in heaven!"[7]

Fourth, biblical scholars have come to appreciate that Jesus' communication form was more what we would today call art than rhetoric. Christ, the ultimate art of the almighty Artist, used stories, metaphors, signs, and symbols to communicate the truth about God.

Matt Knisely has brought all these together, and more, into a book that frames faith and the Christian life less as a worldview and more as a life story. I first met Matt at a conference where he seemed to be the only one present to pick up the real significance of a story I told. After checking him out on social media, I made him an exception to my rule that I only follow my students on Twitter. Followers of Jesus don't so much see different things from anyone else as they see the same things differently. Matt's ability to reframe reality and "see things differently" sparks my own imagination on a daily basis.

Written as if you were sitting across from him at a café, Matt shows us how to approach faith as a photographer approaches a subject or as an artist approaches art. I found it in some ways best compared to the experience of reading the first verse of Psalm 84 in a group with everyone looking at one another: "How lovely is your dwelling place, O Lord Almighty!"

But most importantly, *Framing Faith* shows how to maintain faith's focus on Christ as art, not on the arts of Christ. Two times John the apostle was moved to worship. The angel was so beautiful and awesome and inspiring that John began to bow. But the angel stopped him before he could bend down to worship: "Worship God!"[8] "Worship the Lord in the beauty of holiness."[9]

Framing Faith is not a book on how to art your life better, or how to make worship more vital with better images or higher quality drama. The focus of this book is sharp and zooms in on one thing: how to move faith toward God, and how to better lift Christ up.

Who can forget the logo of Metro-Goldwyn-Mayer movie

productions? It's a roaring lion's head. There is a Latin phrase above the head of the roaring lion: *Ars Gratia Artis.* Translation: art for art's sake. Or a more honest Hollywood translation: art for money's sake.

Written by a highly gifted artist and writer, *Framing Faith* is built upon another motto: *Ars Gratia Dei.* Translation: art for God's sake. Or a more ecclesial translation: art for the glory of God.

—LEONARD SWEET

BEST-SELLING AUTHOR, PROFESSOR

(DREW UNIVERSITY, GEORGE FOX UNIVERSITY),

AND CHIEF CONTRIBUTOR TO SERMONS.COM

INTRODUCTION

You don't make a photograph just with a camera. You bring to the act of photography all the pictures you have seen, the books you have read, the music you have heard, the people you have loved.

—Ansel Adams

I t's time for me to come clean. I have a confession to make. I have a condition. Some might call it a disease; others might call it a disorder; my wife sometimes calls it "living with an artist"—but on a good day she calls it passion. But really, it is this: I am a hoarder. Not a hoarder like you see on TV, with piles of old magazines up to the sky and collections of empty yogurt cups or bottle caps filling the bathtub. I am a hoarder of moments.

I'm passionate about all things that have to do with moments—making them, collecting them, preserving them, remembering them. Moments are what drive me, what fuel what I do and who I am. It's funny how passion makes people think you're crazy. It makes you look like the misfit, the person who marches to the beat of a different drummer. The person who took the road less traveled. The spiritual revolutionary or the eclectic person who runs from painting to photography to writing stories when he gets bored. Truth be told, I'm all of those. Guilty as charged.

I'm that way because I love capturing life. Pen to paper, paint to canvas, subject to sensor, or story to audience. I love bringing stories to life and making them happen for people who wouldn't normally experience them. It's the unique providence of each moment and the story that comes with it that has me enraptured. For me it's all about collecting moments rather than things. Moments get away. They are fleeting and never return. There is something magical about them. I'm constantly collecting thoughts and moments and focusing on fragments to help tell a story.

Pin. Tweet. Clip. Snap. Post. Instagram. Record. Jot. I'm a hoarder of these fleeting moments. I see them as art or beauty rather than some social phenomenon.

If you come over to my house, you won't find mounds of photographs in a mazelike fashion leading from the front door throughout the house, but you will find a curated collection of photographs from my family's life adorning our walls and bookcases. Each photo has its place, its story, and its own distinct and unique character. Some pictures are old, while others are quaint and vestigial. None of the photos was taken in the exact same way, and they were taken in destinations ranging from foreign countries to the park down the street. Different settings were meticulously configured for each setting and scene. As a matter of fact, not one of them was taken with the same camera or lens.

VIEWING LIFE THROUGH THE WRONG LENS

As a photojournalist, I have at least ten different types of cameras and probably twenty or more lenses in addition to hundreds of different pieces of equipment. Why so many? Each piece serves a specific purpose—a purpose that can't be accomplished as well by any other piece. Sure, I could take a portrait shot with a zoom lens, but the resulting image would be more distorted than if I had used a fixed-focal-length or wide-angle lens. And one day it hit me how true these principles are in more areas than just photography.

Have you ever tried to live your life viewed through the wrong lens? Things that belong in the background, tiny and unimportant, are suddenly brought to the front, centered, enlarged, and shown in detail. And the essentials in that snapshot of life are reduced to the periphery, where they can scarcely be seen.

If we are living unintentional lives, not focused on the right things, the picture will be very different than what was intended. We lose sight of what's important. In many cases we are distracted, putting ourselves in autopilot mode and trying to juggle mundane activities along with important activities, such as our relationships with the people around us and, more importantly, our relationship with God. The gift of love is everywhere, but when we are viewing life through the wrong lens, we don't pay attention to its awesome presence.

Instead we flit from activity to activity like a hummingbird, resting momentarily to suck some nectar and enjoyment from one thing before becoming bored and moving on to the next source of pleasure. Things that require focused concentration—quiet times before God, listening to a child's detailed story about his or her day at school, doing meaningful work that contributes to a dream or goal we want to achieve—these things get pushed aside. They don't provide the immediate zings of pleasure that we receive from being retweeted or from getting likes on a photo we posted on Instagram. We seek after the pleasure like a child with a token who wants to play one of those claw crane arcade games. We know the ultimate outcome as we jerk the joystick around in frustration, hope we hold on to, grasp at what could be, but only find ourselves walking away with nothing.

In *Framing Faith* we'll talk about stopping—really stopping—to focus, capture, develop, and savor the moments in life that really matter.

We'll take the time to ask ourselves, "Are we living intentionally? Are we living on purpose? Or are the truly important moments in life passing us by?" I thought I was living intentionally when I began writing this book, but as I finished, I realized I had found a deeper meaning for living in the moment. I want to remember to let myself be intoxicated in the present—the here and the now—so I can see the beauty right in front of me.

SEIZING THE MOMENT

I love using the analogies of photography and videography to explain how we view life, partly because I understand them and am passionate about them and partly because I think they are so applicable. They are art forms that require application of all your gathered knowledge in this world.

Shooting life through a lens truly challenges us to bring out the best we can. That's how passionate, committed, and dedicated we should be if we want to find God and let him enter our lives and frame our faith.

The principle of photography is seizing the moment. *Carpe diem.* It's the seized intentional moments that mean the most. If we continually let go of the moments, we let go of who we are and we lose ourselves.

But seizing the moment is, as most things in life are, easier said than done. Refocusing all our attention on what's really important can't be perfected overnight. As Henri Cartier-Bresson puts it, "Your first 10,000 photographs are your worst."[1] So we can't get discouraged if it takes us until photograph 10,001 to get it right.

This book won't magically solve your focus problems. That's something that only you can do with hard work and determination. But hopefully, it will give you the inspiration, the excitement, and the desire to begin capturing those beautiful moments now . . . today . . . immediately. Not to waste one more day letting life pass you by and going to bed with regrets at what was missed.

FOCUSING OUR FAITH

We live in a culture of distractions. We push ahead on our journey through life. We forge our way through the milestones of our lives, but we don't understand the one thing we should—God is with us every moment of every day. God is what makes the ordinary extraordinary. We need to recognize the moments and the decisive factors we have been given and be able to give the reins to God so the special moments don't slip by. Only in this can we perhaps become what, in truth, we already are: stewards of the moments that have been given to us by God.

In a world moving too fast, this is a book for people seeking to focus their lives, to find a deeper knowledge of God and a more authentic Christian faith. In this modern age, many of us fill every spare moment we have rather than taking an intermission to see the true works of God and realize that he is present in every moment.

The chapters that follow offer a deeper understanding of how the moments in our lives allow God to sculpt us into something beautiful that is our own unique reflection of Christ. Hopefully, we will all see how we need to focus and live in the moment so we can be aware of and uncover the gospel and develop our lives around it. Like a photographer or storyteller, Jesus exhibited time and again how easy it is to capture moments of profound importance simply by noticing, stopping, and responding to his surroundings.

We'll attempt to see biblical truths in a fresh way, allowing us to *really* see them, as if for the first time. I'll ask you probing questions to lead you into a place of honest self-examination, causing you to ask yourself, "Am I listening to God? Is my life God-honoring? Or am I just in this for myself?" My desire is that this provokes you toward reflection, helping to reveal God in everything you see and do.

I hope you will join me in the quest to find a more intense knowledge of God and a more authentic Christian faith in this hurried and busy world. God wants to be present with us through an open and lasting conversation, and it would be shameful for us to ruin the relationship with trivial foolishness when we can feed our souls on the highest thoughts from him.

GOD WANTS US TO FIND PROFOUND
JOY BY SIMPLY THINKING OF HIM . . .
AND IN THOSE MOMENTS, TO TAKE
TIME TO SURVEY OUR SURROUNDINGS,
LOOK THROUGH THE PROPER LENS,
AND BEGIN FRAMING OUR FAITH.

———————

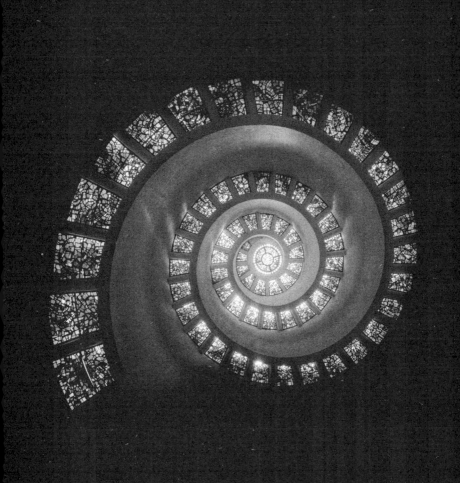

PART ONE

FOCUS

ONE

DISCOVERY

What we see depends mainly on what we look for.
—John Lubbock

I always knew what I wanted to do with my life. I had it all worked out. Perfectly outlined into achievable units of conquest and victory. Methodically calculated down to each and every milestone in my life. I loved telling stories. One day I dreamed of being a storyteller, a weaver of metaphor and narrative, a purveyor of pixels.

Stories have fascinated me for as long as I can remember. I loved when my father would tell us tall tales or wild stories from his childhood—the kind that were so fantastic you wondered if they were really true. My mother told stories just as wonderful as my dad's. She always added another dimension to her narratives by referencing photos stretching all the way back to our family's first photo, which, when I was young, seemed like it was close to the very beginning of time itself.

Along with stories, I began to find myself drawn to photos, and the merging of the medium of photography with story-telling became a real interest. I would immerse myself in large leather-bound photo albums that told the story of our family history. I would slowly thumb through the thick pages riddled with photos with scalloped corners, dissecting each image, gazing into the past, staring at the present, peering into the eyes and lives of my family. Each page I turned revealed stories and images of mythical proportions—it was like I was finding a long-lost treasure. I felt transported to another time and place, another world of infinite possibilities of witnessing, telling, and capturing someone's story. Those albums helped me discover my family and understand myself at a much deeper level.

It was somewhere woven into those early moments that I discovered what I wanted to do with my life. I wanted to help people tell their stories. And not just with pen and paper, but with pictures and sound. I saw that visual stories not only had the ability to comfort, heal, enrage, glorify, and vilify, but they also had a soothing power and effect on people.

The stories I collected for so many years were stories of personal tales about love gone wrong or right—an Elvis imper-sonator who performed at a buffet restaurant in the middle of nowhere, an organ donor's mother meeting the recipient of her son's heart for the first time, or a chance encounter that saved a life. I would dive into every story with poised preci-sion, attempting to capture the heart of each person and taking charge of every word, image, punctuation point, plot twist, pixel, pause, and sentence. I developed, sorted, arranged, and edited ruthlessly to make sure each story revealed something new and displayed truth.

I was obsessed with my work. I have collected and told almost six thousand stories. Most were broken apart into millions of pixels and sent across the airwaves like a cannon shot only to be reassembled in front of a living room audience, staring blankly into the TV in the corner of the room, while others were transmitted via the Internet or live audience. Each story had a purpose, a reason to be told, and it was more than someone's fifteen minutes of fame—or so I would tell myself.

My obsession didn't stop when I left work at night; I was constantly on the lookout for unique stories to tell. Walking into the supermarket I would take a copy of the free paper. I had feeds pulling in stories for me to wade through every morning before I would go to work. I would pick up all the avant-garde magazines on the street corners of every city or town I would visit. I would highlight, cut, paste, fold, and stuff all the interesting and valued assets into a growing folder that I could reference at a moment's notice. I was mainlining narrative.

As the pile of stories grew, so did my career. Everything was right on schedule. I moved from market to market, crisscrossing the United States and the Atlantic Ocean from one city to another. Each move got me closer and closer to my goal—telling bigger and better stories, stories that had more meat and layers than all the others. I was obsessed.

Each story I collected was like an entryway to a new place. Every story, every image, every frame was calling for me to use my imagination and creativity to bring the storyline to life. Ultimately I learned invaluable life lessons from these stories. They grounded me. They nourished me. They inspired me.

WHAT'S MY STORY?

There was only one problem. Those stories weren't *my* story. Yes, many of them became so personal that I almost felt that the stories of other people were, in a sense, my stories as well. And while their stories certainly became a part of me, when it really came down to it, they didn't belong to me.

I remember the day I realized a sobering truth: I had learned how to tell everyone else's story . . . but not my own.

What did it really matter if my story wasn't told? I was telling the stories that really *did* matter—ones that have changed the course of history, ones that fascinate people with their uniqueness, ones that people wanted to hear. My story? Typical. Normal. Standard. Run-of-the-mill. What was the world losing out on by not hearing my story? Not much.

Besides, I had much more to offer as the person *behind* the camera than the person in front of it. We all need to know our role in the world, right? I knew mine. It was storyteller . . . of *other* people's stories. And because their stories were so much better than mine, I didn't see the point in pursuing my own.

But even more than that, I hadn't really allowed myself to explore my own story. If you had commissioned me to create a thirty-minute segment featuring myself, I would have had no idea what to say. There was so much about myself I didn't really even know because I had never taken the time for self-discovery. What was my voice? What was my story? What were my defining moments? It was unsettling to realize that I didn't really know.

The same kind of problem existed for me in my spiritual life. Like the stories of those I'd interviewed, I knew the stories of the Bible by heart. You could name a character, and I'd rattle off the

CliffsNotes of his or her biblical narrative . . . yet I would've been hard-pressed to share how that story had meaningfully shaped my own spiritual narrative. How had these faith adventures and struggles, successes and triumphs, doubts and revelations of so many subjects exposed in Scripture framed the course of my own journey of faith? It was when I realized that the answer to this question carried significant weight that I began to explore my personal story of what God had done in my life, what he was doing in me, and what he wanted to do through me.

EVERY STORY MATTERS

Perhaps the power of biblical stories is not limited to mere bundles of facts and figures of people of old. Perhaps they have power to steer and renew and infuse our life's "film segments" with the divine. Perhaps they help us identify the same elements in our own stories that link us to the rich history and long line of people who lived openly before an ever-present God.

Is it possible that my story of trust is just as important as the prophet Samuel's? That my own struggle to be a disciple is as real as the apostle Peter's? That my own prayers can be as raw and riveting as the ones offered up by King David? That the art and beauty I create can worship God in the same way that the works of Bezalel, chief artisan of the tabernacle, brought glory to him? This realization opened my eyes to the fact that my story—my life—could be just as important to share with the world as others'. And perhaps my passion for photography gives me a unique way to see and frame my faith and will help others begin to tell their stories too.

I can tell you that through the process of writing this story, my story, I have learned a lot about myself. I have learned where my faith finds its roots and the real importance of living my life the way God intended it to be. And perhaps the thing I became most aware of is my need to be present in the moments I am living. As I told more and more stories, God began revealing to me the beauty and power of the moments I was capturing. I began to see how each person's story mattered—including my own.

Our lives are not lived in a vacuum, but rather they are interconnected, woven together, and inseparable. For me to withhold my story would be to rip out a thread from the tapestry of humanity. God has woven me in just as he has woven her in, and him in, and them in . . . and you in.

TWO

ATTENTION

Any man who can drive safely while kissing a pretty girl is simply not giving the kiss the attention it deserves.

—ALBERT EINSTEIN

I look at the world through a unique lens. The photographer/storyteller in me is always looking for the rest of the story. I believe that good photographers have a knack for capturing moments that reveal life nonposed. They can bring into focus defining moments of significance. And what makes these vivid frames resonate is the photographer's attention to the details—to the relationships of light and dark, colors and shapes. These fundamental relationships bring life into focus in real and striking ways.

Each of us holds profound moments within our memory. They are images of significance that have affected us, changed us for good or bad, moved us to laughter or to tears, and defined us. We frame these moments in time as markers of conquest or of extraordinary significance, but we rarely enjoy these moments. Rather, we take pictures, removing ourselves from the moment as if we are capturing history. *Click!* Post to Facebook and Twitter.

There are few things we are less dedicated to than attention. Each of us spends virtually every minute of our day consumed . . . connected . . . and distracted.

Our lives are busy, racing from place to place, barely having time to accomplish everything, rarely having a moment to breathe, and never meeting all of the demands placed upon us. It's as if we have become adverse to margins. We multitask because we think we can get more done. We triple-task because we need to stay in contact. Every gap in our day is filled with information, draining our attention spans and pulling us out of the moment and inserting us into the matrix. We're inattentive . . . preoccupied . . . engrossed . . . oblivious . . . wrapped up in so many things that we are distracted from the moments that are right in front of us. We are disconnected from one another and from our Creator. It's like we are swimming in the ocean while dying of dehydration. We are connected yet alone.

THE THIEF NAMED TECHNOLOGY

We live in a world that seems to be moving at the speed of light. And this world is driven by technology that supposedly makes our lives more comfortable because of the many things we can achieve in a short span of time. That supposedly enriches our relationships because of how many more people we can now connect with and how easy it is to communicate with them. That supposedly makes us happier, more productive, and more efficient, leaving us with more time to do the things that really matter.

But those promises haven't rung true for the grand majority of us. Instead we find ourselves more efficient at "critical tasks" like wishing our Facebook "friends" a happy birthday each day or organizing our music into killer playlists . . . all the while missing out on the faces of those standing right in front of us.

Somehow all of the available technology has turned into a perceived necessity that we, for whatever reason, desperately cling to. And our dependence on it causes us to lose sight of what's really important in life.

The scariest part is we let it happen. Make no mistake—we choose to let this happen. Technology is merely a vehicle that we freely choose to ride on. Whether we enjoy the ride or not, it will ultimately lead us to a place where we're more isolated and alienated—a place where our ancestors have never been. In his article entitled, "Is Facebook Making Us Lonely?" Stephen Marche discusses the limitless and instant comfort technology brings to us. But, he argues, because of it we have become more detached from each other. As Marche says, there is a growing fear that "Facebook is interfering with our real friendships, distancing us from each other, making us lonelier, and that social networking might be spreading the very isolation it seemed designed to conquer."[1]

Experts say that people in our day and age actually become anxious when our brains are not stimulated by technology. As a result, we have become disconnected from other people and events that surround us. We have more "friends" but fewer real friends. More "conversations" but fewer conversations that really matter. Our relationship pool has grown much, much wider but also much, much shallower. Our real relationships are the ones that fill us, that truly satisfy us.

If we describe our relational needs in terms of physical hunger, the majority of the "friends" we interact with via technology fill us up the way an iced mocha cappuccino does—an initial burst of energy and pleasure that crashes shortly after. What our soul really craves is a solid meal—interactions with actual friends or family that take time, an investment of emotional energy, planning, thought, and focus.

But our society has begun to treat our relational needs much the same way we've come to treat our physical needs. When we're hungry, rather than take the time to cook a well-balanced, filling meal, we rush to grab something out of the freezer that we can quickly nuke and then eat while watching TV or finishing up some work. And when we're relationally hungry, so often rather than sitting down with our children or spouse to hear about their day or setting up a dinner date with a good friend, we open Facebook or Twitter and peruse through the recent posts of the day, stopping to click "like" or shoot off some quick replies. Or we look to see if a picture we posted to Instagram earlier that day has been commented on much—and if it was, that temporarily fills us . . . until we close our computer and crawl into bed with the same dissatisfied, empty feeling that we went to bed with the day before.

When it comes down to it, technology has created a culture of distraction, keeping us stimulated by things that don't really matter. This is far from ideal. When we start to fill our minds and hearts with voices that don't really add meaning, over time we'll silence the voice of the only One who does.

We begin life with nothing but humble rations from a loving Creator. As infants, we are given the gift of connection to our mother. We are presented the gift of relationship and love from our new family. The simplest of things were gifts for a reason. But at some point in our lives we lose control of what's happening to us and around us, and we begin to become controlled by the need for things to occupy our time and attention, the need to acquire more and more in the pursuit of happiness. This is life's greatest lie.[2]

DISTRACTIONS AND DEFINING MOMENTS

It's as if we are searching, looking for something, and the more we look, the more we move into emptiness *because we lack defining moments*. Despite our best efforts, our attention seems to be held captive by communicating in 140 characters or less, status updates, short blog posts, apps, hashtags, and text messages with ridiculous abbreviations . . . SMH! It's like watching an out-of-control freight train headed for derailment, and we cannot look away. We are wired to crave the temporary satisfaction from writing e-mails, crafting tweets, returning calls, downloading music, playing games, checking out websites, sending text messages, and taking photos of our food. They are the hooks that enrapture us. They are the casino slot machines that keep us moving from one machine to the next, ultimately resulting in our anxiety when we are left to face the world unstimulated.

As a photojournalist, if I were to approach my subjects in

the same frenetic, distracted manner, not only would my career be short-lived but the stories and images would be surface and meaningless. And if this level of focus matters so much in my work relationships, why would I think it is any different in other areas of my life?

I need to be honest; I have terrible anxiety. Worry invades my consciousness all the time. From my perspective, it feels as if the world is accelerating and becoming much more than I can handle. There are times I wake up in the morning feeling extremely overwhelmed with thoughts racing through my mind, and it takes me an hour to get ready without feeling rushed. I can't even enjoy my day because anxiety arrests me when I think about all of the tasks I have to accomplish, even if some of the tasks should ideally be enjoyable. The lack of attention to the moments that are all around me is evident. I wish that the world would just slow down to about half the speed it is functioning at right now.

I feel my life is measured by small units of time that give me nothing left for hobbies or family, and I am nostalgic for simpler times. What brings me even more unrest is looking at my children. It seems like yesterday I was holding them in my hands and now they're holding iPhones and iPads in theirs. When I talk to them, they rarely raise their heads from their electronic devices to make eye contact.

My wife and I have worked very hard to correct this. We now create breaks in our day by limiting screen time, and we have a strict rule that we do not use any devices whenever we sit at the dinner table. We do this to disconnect from the distractions and connect to the things that matter—relationships. We work really hard to limit digital interactions, forcing creativity, personal interaction, and ultimately, margins.

I have breakfast with my kids every morning, and we talk about the day ahead, goof off, and just stare sleepy-eyed at each other. But a recent morning was different. I don't remember exactly why I did what I did—it most likely was something pressing regarding work that could have waited—but I came to breakfast with my laptop. I sat on one side of the table, and my son and daughter sat, eagerly awaiting our morning conversation, on the other side. But between us was a digital barrier.

I don't remember that morning's conversations at all, yet I can recount with clarity the conversations from the previous morning and the morning before that. I found out later from my wife that my son had been trying in earnest to get my attention. He had been elevating his voice, making faces, asking about my day—the things we normally would do. But I sat there, zombie-like, seduced by the electromagnetic emissions of my laptop.

I didn't think much of it at the time, but at some point my day began catching up to me and I remembered that moment. It's a moment I wish I could forget. A moment I wish I could go back and fix. A moment where my actions were saying, "My digital connections are more important than the people in front of me." The reality is, I'm not alone in that experience. And somehow I think we were created for more.

God gives each of us divine moments. Despite the fast rate at which we live our lives, he is faithful to give us new chances to be reminded. But are we paying attention? Do we have enough will, enough strength, enough dissatisfaction with the current state of things to stop this runaway train that we've let our lives become and say to the conductor, "I want off! I refuse to let my life fly past me anymore without really seeing it. Without really experiencing it. Without really savoring it."

Does your life feel like a runaway train? Are you so occupied with life's distractions that you're looking down at what's in your hand, occasionally lifting your eyes to the windows and gazing wistfully at the scenery whizzing past you?

We like to think we are fully immersed in the here and now, aware of our surroundings and the moments around us—but we are more tuned out then we've ever been. We are deeply absorbed, briefly having fun but ultimately burdened and stressed out by trying to keep up with all the different technologies we have at our disposal. Our emotions and moments are held captive the faster and more frantically we flip and flick through all of our gadgets, trying in vain to give our full attention to three or four different things at the same time. We've lost control of what thing or which one we should pay attention to. Finally, out of desperation and overstimulation, we cry for help.

Let me be the voice that cuts through the noise in your head that is keeping you from hearing the truth. A voice that I have needed so many times in my life to stop me from running at a nonsensical pace.

Look up.

Put down what's in your hand.

Stop the train.

Yes, sometimes we need to get on the train to get from point A to point B. But we were never created to live as permanent seat occupants on a train that never reaches its final destination. We weren't created for the train; the train was created for us. Putting it another way, we weren't created for technology; technology was created for us.

I'm a realist. There are moments that we need to move fast, and honestly, I can't imagine living without some of the key pieces of technology I rely on. I'll never be a horse-and-buggy kind of guy, even though I grew up in the heart of Amish paradise. I love a good, fast train ride to get me quickly and efficiently where I need to go. But I'm learning to look out the windows, to talk to my seatmates, to stop and drink a cup of coffee that's offered to me, and most importantly, to get off the train when it's time. To be more aware of the moments and experiences and people around me who may just become a part of my next defining moment. Or perhaps I'll become a part of theirs.

How do we keep ourselves from getting distracted? With so much going on around us, do we even know what to pay attention to? God calls on us every single day. How so? Every day we stretch the muscles of our body when we wake up. Every morning we have a brief moment to sip a hot cup of coffee. Every morning we squint at the bright rays of the sun hitting our eyes. Every day the cool water splashes our sleepy face. Every time someone greets us, "Good morning!" Every time we see that sweet smile on our loved one's face. Every time we decide to help someone who asked us for a favor. These are just some of the many brief moments in which God calls on us. If you'll become aware, these are the very moments when we have thoughts uncontaminated with technology's distractions. And these thoughts so often are God's voice speaking to us. Do we hear him?

THE BARRIERS WE BUILD

This story is no different in our relationship with God. Just like I do with my children, God wants a deep relationship with us. He is the one pursuing that relationship. God passionately pursues us, wanting to spend time with us. But instead of answering his affection, we so often build barriers between ourselves and his greatness. It's like when God gave the Israelites the Ten Commandments—their response was to have Moses speak to God and relay the message back to them, rather than directly encountering God themselves.[3] Moses became a barrier, cutting God off from his people. God's desire was to have a direct relationship with his people, but they constantly refused him.

To this day, we continually build barriers between ourselves and God. By letting ourselves get distracted, by not being attentive, we lose some important elements of our existence. We ignore the ingredients God has used in creating our unique selves. And we suppress real human connection when we prioritize other things over the people right in front of us, ultimately preventing us from understanding anything or anyone at a profound level. If we don't know how to go deep, then we will never be able to truly know ourselves and other people. This has serious implications for how we can know God. God wants our attention in the midst of this hurried and busy world. He wants us to frame our lives around him and the moments he has created for us.

We are busying ourselves to death.

Our minds are lost.

Our walk has been disturbed.

God wants us to shed our desires, our stuff, and our distractions so that we can find him.

Our greatest and most destructive sin may just be "being busy." It is robbing us of the moments right in front of us. We have to learn to resist the anxious momentum of the world. We need to see quietness and rest as our salvation. Christ is our rest, our peace. He is the gaps and moments of our days. He is there to free us from the exhaustion, to direct our passions and lives. If we let our minds be consumed and abused by the world's stuff, we will lose our ability to know God and show him to the world and our families.

And when we take the time to stop and rest, to stop and focus, to stop and purposefully decide what we will choose to do with our lives—we will begin to engage God and those around us in more intentional ways, and our lives will begin to fill with the kinds of experiences and stories that really matter. Stories full of purpose.

THREE

PURPOSE

"Thou shalt not" is soon forgotten, but "Once upon a time" lasts forever.

—PHILIP PULLMAN

H ow many times have you been intrigued by a good story? Take a second to think about this, because I'm pretty sure it has happened more than you initially realize. How many times have you started reading a good book that you couldn't put down or become so enthralled in a movie that you couldn't tear yourself away for even a second to refill your popcorn? Think about how often you have been inspired to push yourself harder after hearing a story of someone overcoming all the odds, or changed your mind after experiencing a powerful, convincing narrative. Or think about the time you stared at a photograph, eyes locked onto the subject, swept up by the story it was telling. We find these stories and images fascinating because we are filled with curiosity. Stories change the way we act, think, and feel.

We are natural storytellers; we are drawn to story like moths to a flame. We invite others to be part of our story time and time again. Photographers seek to tell a story with a single image—capturing a mere fraction of a second that records an exchange now frozen in time to be shown and retold time and time again. These captured moments are healing; they reveal fugitive truths, a vast range of emotion, and our souls, all in one decisive moment. These moments have a purpose. They have a story to tell.

Of course the gift of a good story is something that doesn't just happen—it takes a good storyteller to weave prose with suspense. It takes a great photographer to anticipate a decisive moment, knowing when to release the shutter and capture a photograph that conveys emotion, mood, narrative, ideas, and messages in a single image. It takes work. To grab hold of and keep your audience's attention, you need to be intentional about learning how to tell stories and practicing your craft.

But the real magic of the story happens in the relationship between the image and its audience. Story is communal. It's not something that's solitary or trapped in a vacuum that no one can experience or live out. No, the act of storytelling can only happen when the story, storyteller, and audience join together and that connection is poised in the middle of two distinct worlds—the world of the story (the imagined) and the actual here-and-now world (the physical location).

MY GRANDFATHER, THREE FINGERS
OF SCOTCH, AND NEEDLEWORK

We live in an environment rich with story. Stories are contagious—tell a story, take a photo, and if it resonates, it'll spread. They demand to be retold, time and time again. Stories reverberate and embed themselves in our shared memory. They may not immediately change our lives, but they descend deep into our fabric and rest there. They settle and grow and then, when the time is just right, they begin to do their work. Stories influence. They motivate, and they direct us from the outside in, surfacing and returning to remembrance as we experience new stories and life experiences. Stories shape us.

Our lives revolve around stories, and for as long as I can remember, I have been enamored with their power. I believe family provides the network of the deepest and most important stories of society. Better than any family heirloom, stories are one of the greatest gifts we can give to our children. Stories are equipment for life.[1]

My grandfather really knew how to tell a story. For him, telling stories was like delicate needlework; every word, every pronunciation, and every intonation was carefully placed. He knew the art of storytelling. He understood what drew people to a story and what inspired them, and he always wove in a clever twist. We had a saying in our family: "When D. B. Spatz talks, we listen."

Grandfather spent his life as an engineer, primarily designing tanks. The word *engineer* defined him to a T. He loved examining things, trying to understand how something worked, what made it tick. If he didn't know the answer, he would find it and then devour the information so he could recall it at a moment's notice. He also observed and studied and taught us, his family. And he knew us as well as anything.

I remember the last story he told me; it was the night before he passed. He had been sick for a while and was in a hospital bed. His body was failing, but his mind was as sharp as ever. Grandfather leaned forward so I could hear him, his thick eyebrows arched, and his head turned. With a quick gesture he raised his right arm and motioned for me to come closer. As he sat there wearing his enormous glasses, his cologne hanging in the air, he began to tell me the story of how he met my grandmother (who had passed away almost a year prior to that date). It was a story I had heard many times, but my grandfather told it from a slightly different angle each time so you could always learn something new and notice something fresh.

But the beginning . . . the beginning was always the same: "It was our first date for your grandmother and me. She was so beautiful and intimi*dating*," he chuckled.

"First dates are the be-all and the end-all, the beginning of something wonderful or the end of one that never was . . . I'd had a lot of never was. We went to this quaint restaurant, and I was making sure I did everything right to impress her. I was on time picking her up, opened doors, and paid attention to every word she said. And then disaster hit. About halfway through the meal, I went to cut my shrimp when it went flying across the restaurant. Those things are slippery devils," he said.

He continued, "I was devastated and figured that was the last date I'd have with this beautiful woman. When I dared look up at her, my cheeks blazing with embarrassment, I saw her face, lips pursed tight, eyes bright and dancing, shoulders shaking. She finally couldn't hold it in anymore and burst out laughing . . . and I joined her.

"The moral of the story," he exclaimed, raising his pointer finger in the air, "is that your grandmother was a very forgiving woman and taught me that laughing at ourselves is okay, but when we invite others to laugh with us it's a gift."

I remember sitting next to him, an adult fascinated and entertained by his stories. They had a comforting and almost healing effect on me. They were real. Full of humility. His stories allowed me to relive the milestones and wonderful times of my childhood. As Robert McKee so aptly says, "Stories are the creative conversation of life itself; they are the currency of human contact."[2] I would add that stories are the currency of the Knisely family. Not the "once upon a time" kind of stories, but *real* family stories.

If you had asked my grandfather what the formula of a great story is, he would have probably answered, "Three fingers of Scotch," and laughed. Then he would have thought for a moment, leaned in, and told you that you needed to watch your interactions with people—specifically, when you are telling a story to your audience, notice when they react positively to that story. He knew if he got a positive reaction from his audience he had a story that he could retell without much tweaking. He would have then told you that you needed four things to tell a great story: attention, conflict, resolution, and a nice big bow at the end. He had a way of examining all the parts of a story carefully, just as a watchmaker would examine fine Swiss craftsmanship. Storytelling was not some kind of social movement for him; it was who he was.

LONELY IN A CROWDED ROOM

Somewhere, storytelling has become a movement. Why? What is it about story in this particular point in human history and culture that makes it resonate with so many people? Something my grandfather knew inherently but could never verbalize was that we were in the twilight of communicating relationally, face-to-face, heart to heart, person to person, flesh to flesh. Seth Godin refers to this as the "connection revolution."[3]

What my grandfather knew to do, and something I believe culture is currently trying to do, was to hold on to and place more value on the one human gift that cannot be widgetized and homogenized into mechanized technology: emotion.

I remember a time when my grandfather picked up my iPad, flipping it around in his hands, trying to understand it, and said, "What happened to people making more of their own things? It's beautiful . . . but it's an attention zapper."

He was referring to a time when people drafted stories from their life experiences and told them to one another regularly because that was what entertained us. They weren't today's uploaded, reengineered, impersonal stories. My grandfather knew that sharing stories connects us to one another; our stories forge relationships and bring a strong sense of intimacy and self. We have replaced many of these human connections with digital connections. Let's face it: at times, these devices seem to do everything for us. Yet these kinds of connections have left us lonely.

Lonely
in a crowd
of thousands
of *friends*.

My grandfather believed that we've muted the colors found in the fabric of our Creator. That we've taken the brilliant canary yellows of shared human joys and toned them down to pallid yellow emoticons. And the deep midnight blues of pain and sadness? They've become washed out and dulled, like the color of the sky in an overexposed photo that has lost its shadows and depth. The bright sunset red of passion that burns steadily and deeply, carrying a person past initial excitement and through to completion? It's been reduced to a short burst of color that quickly fades to the pale shade of fizzless champagne.

He didn't believe that we'd utterly gone to sleep—after all, we still search for things to devote ourselves to. But that's just it: we often search for things rather than people.

SHARING OUR STORIES WITH THE NEXT GENERATION

The Old Testament, by and large, was passed down from generation to generation verbally. The Jewish people sat around and told redemption stories. Then their children did the same thing twenty years later.

Repeat.

Repeat.

God designed us to be relational. From the beginning of time, God intended for us to enjoy companionship. He did not intend us to be lonely, isolated, and switched off from one another.[4] God has provided us with a priceless gift. A perfect gift. A perpetual gift that keeps giving. In other words, God's greatest gift to us is relationship.

More importantly, God intended for us to share stories. When Israel crossed the Jordan River, Joshua called out twelve men from each tribe and directed them to cross and for each tribe to take up a stone from the middle of the river as a living marker for their children. The stones were meant to be a reminder—they tell a visual story of when the flow of the Jordan River stopped in front of the ark of the covenant as the Israelite priests, holding it by poles on their shoulders, stepped with it into the water. The stones were purposefully placed where they camped as a permanent memorial for the people of Israel to recount that story for generations upon generations.[5]

God knew that stories connect us to one another and connect each generation to the next. Sharing stories helps the next generation know what one went through or experienced so that when, and if, they come to a point in their lives where they are faced with a similar situation, they will have an idea of how to face it.

That's really what history is. History is a collection of our stories, as humankind, from which we can learn, grow, be entertained, feel inspired, and ultimately feel a connection to those who have gone before us and have lived lives worth remembering.

The foundation of our history here, in America, is based around generations of Native Americans. There is this one particular band of Native Americans called the Lakota, who lived on the northern plains of North America. They had a unique way of recording their history: they kept track of the year from one winter to the next, from the first snowfall to the next. These accounts were called *waniyetu wowapi*, or "winter counts."[6]

What was special about these chronicles was how they were recorded. Within each tribe, the elders would review the past year, come up with the most significant events that defined the year for them, and combine the events into a single image that they then released to the keeper of the winter count. It was the job of the keeper to present the tribe's narrative of their life together that year into an image to be drawn or painted on to buffalo skin or deer hide to record each passing year. The keeper created a collection of images that would encapsulate a report of the tribe's history. The keeper was responsible for recounting the visual narrative.

Those Native Americans realized the power of storytelling; they realized that images were a way to portray their story and preserve the memory of their narrative in living form. Just like the twelve stones taken from the Jordan River, the winter count spoke to generations upon generations of the lives their ancestors had experienced. They were emotional stories that connected people from one age with those who had gone before them.[7]

Stories such as those found in Scripture are never simply about imparting information or reminding people of previous experiences. They are never about providing historical facts for their own sake. The purpose of story is to generate a relationship—to promote trust and intimacy, to gain acceptance, and to have an emotionally healing experience.

We can argue statistics, we can debate theories, and we can challenge philosophies, but there is something about a person's raw, honest story that connects with us on a deeper level and gets us out of our head and into our heart. You might tell me you read that 50 percent of Christians say they are happier now than before entering into a relationship with Jesus or that you believe Christians, in general, live more fulfilled lives, or you can read me an excerpt from a book, or quote a respected pastor or theologian to illustrate your point. But none of those things will move me as much as you—just you—looking at me with truth in your eyes and sharing your story of when you let Jesus enter into the broken mess your life had become and how he filled your empty heart with his unconditional love and redeemed you. No statistic can ever carry more power than a person's true story told with authenticity.

My grandfather taught me that sharing our stories is really sharing our faith in what God is doing in our lives. Our stories connect with others at the heart level, making a connection that moves well beyond intellect to life change. The purpose of story is to shape and direct the lives of God's people.

As we go about our daily lives, let's not forget to share the story of God's work in our lives, fully aware that it is he who is orchestrating it. And let's take care to not share only the pretty, edited, CliffsNotes versions, but the honest, imperfect moments of our lives where we messed up and God saved the day. Because the real story is always the best story.

FOUR

PERFECTION

Where there is perfection there is no story to tell.

—BEN OKRI

I am always searching for the perfect moment. You know, the one where fate, destiny, the right light, and the perfect subject matter all collide at just the right instant in time. *Click!* I've dreamed about taking a perfect picture. I've researched techniques and purchased better and more precise equipment. I've even gone as far as learning how to heighten my senses so I would be able to anticipate that decisive moment when the shutter opens and closes, in a blink of an eye. These things can both help and hinder the photographer on his quest to take the perfect photo.

Photographers spend a lifetime chasing perfection, trying to duplicate or even outdo one another by capturing bigger and more poignant moments. We have an inner voice pushing us to constantly look underneath things, to see what's hiding in the back alleys or even what stories are in front of us. It's like we are on a never-ending treasure hunt, searching for the Holy Grail. Few have come to realize that a great photograph is not made by the lens or the camera, or even by the software you may use to manipulate the end result—rather, great photographs are made by the moment that is captured in an instant. The sad reality of all this effort is that no matter how much planning, preparation, or focus you give it, there is no such thing as the perfect photo. Artistic perfection does not exist, no matter how fervently we strive after it.

A STORYTELLER FROZEN INTO SILENCE

One Wednesday night, several years ago, a missionary stepped onto the stage of our church. He had recently returned from Africa, where he and his wife had been serving for the last four years. Being a missionary was relatively new to him. He wasn't one of those lifers who had been in the field for the last twenty years. Rather, he had traded the air-conditioned offices of his company's finance department, where he had worked for the bulk of his career, for the heat and discomfort of far-off Mozambique.

As he stepped up on the stage, music played and images of the work he and his wife had been doing in Mozambique appeared on the screens. The room came to life, and I could almost imagine I was sitting in one of his chapel services in Africa. All of us in the room were drawn in by the moving pictures on the screen . . . but then, something happened. Suddenly the presentation stopped on one of the images and refused to move forward. The screen froze. Nothing happened. And then we noticed the missionary was also frozen.

We all sat in silence, waiting in anticipation for it to start up again . . . but nothing. Was it his computer? Did it freeze? Was it the projection technology? Or was it the missionary himself? Did he forget what he was going to say? Had his thoughts frozen on his lips before they had a chance to come out? Why wasn't he saying something? Didn't he realize that he had to keep going? That everyone was looking at him, watching and waiting?

I'm not sure what happened or what was going on in his mind as he stood there, immobile. Perhaps we were the first church on his speaking circuit. Maybe he hadn't slept well in the unfamiliar bed of his hotel room the night before. Maybe the pressure of needing to effectively communicate what their mission overseas was, got to him. Whatever it was, the man choked.

There was a painfully awkward silence as he stood there, speechless. The silence continued as seconds passed while we watched him stand there, frozen by the icy grip of fear. For those of us watching, those initial seconds felt like minutes—for him, I'm sure it was hours—disturbed by not a sound except a few ahs, ums, and the clearing of his throat. At first, the room of almost four hundred people was as quiet as a falling leaf. Time felt as if it stood still as tiny sounds began to emerge—coughs from the back row, the creaking of the wooden pews as those in the room shifted in their seats uneasily.

I sat in the balcony, holding my breath. Hoping. Waiting. And silently praying that this noble man would be able to collect his thoughts. Then suddenly his wife's voice shot out like a cannon, breaking the silence from her perch on the front pew and coming to his rescue. "Jambo!" she said (which means *hello* in Swahili), as she stood up and walked onstage. She took the microphone and gave about a one-minute overview of their work in Mozambique before the pastor retook the stage—a far cry from the larger, more in-depth presentation the two of them had planned.

His big moment was suddenly over. His one chance to connect with the people in our congregation about the mission he was so passionate about . . . gone. An opportunity he had worked so hard to gain . . . lost.

After the service was over, I found this missionary sitting down, slumped in perceived defeat behind the table the church had set up for him to use to display his information. His head was in his hands as he sat on a chair, hidden from the congregants who might want more information about their mission.

I sat down beside him, and my shoulder bumped into his. I introduced myself and then began to tell him a story of something similar that had happened to me. Almost ten years earlier, I had been in Springfield, Missouri, working as a reporter for a local television station. I explained to him that up until that point in my career I had tried to stay invisible by hiding behind a camera.

It was my first week on the job, and my photographer and I really outdid ourselves; we fed back a beautifully shot story that we were both proud of. The only catch was that this time, they wanted me to speak in front of the camera. I stood there, calmly waiting, breathing in confidence and out determination. My hair looked good, the live shot had been tuned in perfectly, and I had my intro down pat. Ron Burgundy would have been proud.

I remember hearing the anchor in my IFB (the earpiece news

correspondents wear so they can hear any communication from the producer or anchors), "Our Matt Knisely has been following the story and has more . . . Matt?" I went to open my lips, but instead of my carefully rehearsed intro, all that came out was a slight puff of air. There I was, staring at the camera with the small crowd of onlookers snickering as the light from the camera glared in my face and my producer yelled in my ear. After a few awkward moments, they dumped out of my live shot and began playing my story instead. That moment was a cross between a deer caught in headlights and an out-of-body experience.

Looking visibly more relaxed, the missionary laughed as I finished the story and said, "Wow. I only froze in front of a few hundred people, not several thousand."

STORYTELLING IS MESSY

The problem with this missionary and myself lay with both of us wanting to tell a great story. Both of us passionately wanted to be master storytellers, weaving plots and storylines that would keep our audiences hooked and wanting more. But as we sat there together behind his missions display, I began to think about why we both had failed so badly when we had tried so fervently.

For many of us, simply opening our mouths to talk in front of others seems terrifying. And as if that isn't enough, good storytelling requires having an understanding of who your audience is so you can communicate in a way that connects with them. Then you need to take all of that and somehow put it into a neat package and deliver it in the form of a story.

Telling stories can be scary. And sometimes we trip and fall on our faces when we stick out our necks and share our experiences. If perfection is our goal, we will rarely achieve it in our own eyes. But we can't let this discourage us or silence our voices. The reality is that neither the words *impossible* nor *easy* aptly describe the art of storytelling.

Somewhere in the midst of me sharing these new thoughts with the missionary, I realized something that had been staring me in the face nearly every day for my entire career: storytelling is *messy*. Yes, messy! Stories in their context are primitive. Usually, the most powerful stories are ones that are authentic, honest, vulnerable, and personal. When anxiety is mixed with a motivation to bring a slick message, presentation, or story, the beautiful simplicity of what we have to share is often undermined. The reality is if your motivation is to try to make perfectly polished and packaged stories, and you allow your desire for perfection to dominate you, this desire will undermine what you're ultimately trying to accomplish, which is to help your audience resonate with the humanity of the story.

The chaotic.

The raunchy.

The sensual.

The sloppy.

The emotional.

The true.

We must take a stand against the winds of all of the strongest perceived truths and notions we have of story. A story unravels the highs, the lows, the difficult decisions, the accomplishments, and it takes its audience into a deeper meaning of the narrative. Stories help tell our most important truths of our own human experiences. Stories are messy because the human experience is messy. As storytellers we are often nervous about sharing the *real* experiences of *real* people and their *real* stories because when you tell their stories as they truly are, they become less formulaic than we want them to be. But storytellers deal in the currency of these moments; after all, a story without moments is a like a treasure without coins.

All of this is really hard to admit when your personality is the type that wants to fix things, to be in control, and most of all, to create flawless work. The reality that hit me was that both this missionary and I were fighting perfectionism. As artists and communicators, we are passionate about the "niceness" of our delivery—in this case conveying a well-told story. We find ourselves constantly in "aesthetic arrest" in a perfectionistic culture as we try to achieve beauty in everything we do. But sooner or later, every person trying to create something comes face-to-face with and battles the vicious monster known as perfectionism.

DREADS, PATCHOULI, AND SETTING THE WORLD ON FIRE

When I think of perfection, I think of a beautifully shot sequence that reveals hope, or a riveting story of how missionaries in Africa are making a difference one tribe at a time. But somewhere along the line my desire to do amazing work can actually stunt my progress. And the same thing happens to you; we psych ourselves out.

Storytelling, in a lot of cases, is organic—it happens naturally. The term *organic* brings to mind images of Whole Foods, patchouli, eclectic bohemians in dreads, Birkenstocks, wheatgrass, and dairy-free cheese. But the term can also be applied to storytelling. Just as we've seen a trend in society's desire for all things organic and natural, I think we've also seen a trend in people's desire for authenticity, honesty, and openness in communication. The phrases *all natural, keepin' it real,* and *raw and unedited* hold appeal for many of us who are looking for the "real deal"—something or someone we can relate to. People are drawn to so-called reality shows and blogs that promise to tell what's *really* going on. When it comes down to it, we crave the truth. The stripped-down, unedited, unbiased facts.

Stories need to be flawed. If they're all clean and shiny, we don't believe them. Even children know there's a stepmother in every Cinderella story, a Mount Doom to conquer before Middle Earth can be free, and puzzles and riddles to solve on the way to owning the Chocolate Factory. Stories without struggles feel empty and hollow. We resonate with pain, with challenges, with mistakes and mess-ups. As Americans, we have a history of rooting for the underdog. We love deeply flawed characters we know have great goodness hidden within them. Perhaps that's why Jean Valjean's character in *Les Misérables* is considered one of the greatest of all time. Or why we are so moved by Oprah's journey from troubled teen, abused and molested, involved in drugs, sex, and alcohol, to self-made billionaire philanthropist and global influencer.

We love these types of stories because we identify with the imperfections. We see the flaws in our own character yet hope and pray that God can somehow make something great out of us. We think, *If God could use that person, perhaps he could use me.* And *that* is why we must share more of our stories—more of

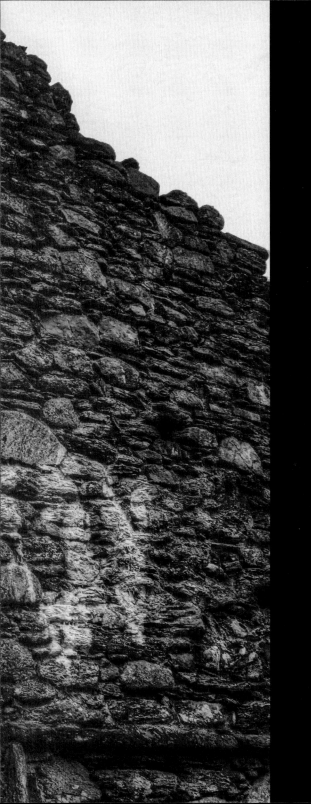

the flaws, more of the mistakes, more of the fall-flat-on-our-face moments where we messed things up almost beyond repair.

But we don't leave it there. Because a story that ends in failure, that terminates with tragedy, is not one that inspires. And it's not our story! If we really look at our lives, we can see how God has made beauty out of our ashes, how he has exchanged joy for our sadness, and how he has placed praise on our lips instead of grief. To share only the pain of our stories is to leave them incomplete. We must share how God redeemed our failures, how we learned to laugh at ourselves, how we learned life-changing lessons through those moments that have shaped who we are today. And when we are as open about our failures as our successes, we free people to become the people God has created them to be. To realize they don't have to fit into a mold of perfection but can trust God to help them be their best selves—even as they trip and mess up along the way.

St. Catherine of Siena is known for saying, "If you are what you should be, you will set the world on fire."[1] Admit it, some things are more easily said than done, even when it comes to becoming who God has created us to be. While this is our challenge in life, we all struggle in some way or another to live that very statement out because we all see the messy details and problems in our own lives; we're flawed.

Weak.

Imperfect.

Fallen.

Human.

Understanding the way God structures things is no different than understanding the true structure of the perfect story; it's *not* easy. But I believe that he specifically created us with good and evil in us—flawed so we could grow. Think about it. If you never felt pain and hurt, how would you know love and joy when you felt it? How can you grow if you don't learn from your mistakes and the mistakes of others?

THE MASTER STORYTELLER AND HIS FLAWED CHARACTERS

The notion that God is a storyteller never really crossed my mind (maybe it wasn't supposed to) until that moment I sat talking to the missionary. It was like one of those moments in an M. Night Shyamalan movie where the story and plot collapse on itself, revealing something that had been sitting before your eyes the whole time. The stories that run through the sixty-six books of the Bible are filled with moments of hope, despair, joy, brokenness, challenge, darkness, pain, happiness, drunkenness, and faith. The importance of these moments and what they reveal are God's revelation for his people. They show that the story doesn't end with the Bible. God's story of love, rescue, resurrection, and renewal is progressive and is really our story—and he is inviting us to participate.

In the stories about David and Jonathan or Joseph and his brothers we begin to see not only how God weaves story, but also his theme of loving the imperfect. Page after page of the Bible tells a story of unworthy, inadequate individuals who certainly didn't have it all together. Take Sarah, for example. She laughed at God's promise to give her a son in her old age.[2] Though in contrast, God used Sarah to begin a family that would become the nation of Israel and his chosen people. Then there was

David, a "peeping Tom," the "premeditated sinner" (not sure how I missed this in Sunday School growing up), who had a man killed in a cover-up after he committed adultery with his wife.[3] Yet, David went on to write seventy-three of the 150 Psalms. His writings reveal and portray a raw and honest faith, full of joy one moment and full of angst the next; and he is known as being "a man after God's own heart."[4]

And who can forget Moses? His story is one wild ride. Nearly murdered baby to adopted Egyptian prince to accused murderer to fugitive to shy sheepherder to stuttering spokesman to leader of all Israel. Time and time again, God uses imperfect people to fulfill His perfect plan.

Step back a little further and look at what ultimately landed Jesus on a cross: it was his idea that people—no matter how common, broken, or messed up—could be considered godly. That idea drove people mad and is why Jesus made enemies, because he was challenging the status quo and loving the imperfect ones.

PERFECTION IS AN UNATTAINABLE GOAL

My life has been about fighting against the imperfect. Warring with weakness. For years, I pledged myself to the pursuit of perfection. During my career in broadcast news, I worked every day to put together a story that connected with each viewer by evoking emotions of sadness, anger, or love. I wanted each story to hit a certain pace, to be told from the perspective of a central character, and I worked diligently not to rush to the punch line. In the end, I would grapple with the incredibly difficult task of making sure the story I was telling would point people toward a desired conclusion yet give them the freedom to draw the conclusion themselves. My compulsiveness into indefectibility quickly went downhill from there.

My perfectionism regarding creating a great story all came to light that fateful night as I stood in front of the camera stunned and at a loss for words. As I told the missionary at our church, I'll never forget the anchor saying, "Our Matt Knisely has been following the story and has more . . . Matt? . . . Matt? Can you hear me?"

I have replayed that moment in the theater of my mind a thousand times or more. The anxiety it brings hangs like a dark, impenetrable cloud. Why? Because I set the bar in everything I do extremely high and always put my best foot forward to achieve those goals. My wife will tell you, I commit extensive amounts of attention and time to my work and the things I'm passionate about to protect my high standards. And that drive for excellence motivates me to go the second mile, never giving in and never giving up.

I was a year or two into my role as director of photo-journalism for the FOX-owned-and-operated television station in Minneapolis. I had been tasked with rebuilding the pho-tography and editing staff and making it one of the best in the country. It was a daunting assignment. And it was hard work. A *lot* of hard work. How hard? Minneapolis is regarded as one of the best markets in television for quality and journalistic excel-lence when it comes to in-depth, people-oriented, hard-news storytelling. You could switch the channel between the local CBS, NBC, and ABC stations and see award-winning stories on a nightly basis. They were stories that revealed the humanity of the day's events through impeccable reporting and photography.

For those of us in television news it was like the Sundance Film Festival every night. Each station's accomplishments read like the World Series winnings of the New York Yankees, St. Louis Cardinals, and Oakland Athletics.

So taking a station not on the grid was obviously hard work—kind of like trying to lead the Tampa Bay Rays into winning the World Series. The lucky thing I had going for me was a constant flood of résumés from photojournalists in other markets trying to break into the majors. I slowly grew the staff from ten photographers to more than thirty-two. My days were spent mentoring and critiquing the staff. Pushing for high quality. Relentlessly talking about perfect story structure. Holding seminar sessions on lighting and storytelling on the weekends.

But the biggest hurdle was breaking down the personal walls that divided the newsroom and staff. I spent every waking moment pouring myself into my staff and into my role on the management team, all to raise standards and quality of our visual product. Eventually, ratings went up and we went from being a blip in the ratings to the second-place spot. I continued to pour myself into the team, spending weekends with them researching, shooting, and editing stories. I wanted each staff member to be passionate about telling stories through compelling pictures and sound. I taught them to understand that people feel emotional about their own communities, so capturing that emotion was key.

Then one cold March morning all our hard work paid off. We were awarded the title of being one of the greatest photo staffs in the country that year by the National Press Photographers Association. Shortly after that, I was at a dinner with my parents and went into a panic attack, which at the time felt more like a heart attack. On my return to work, the vice president of news told me he appreciated my desire for excellence and perfectionism and how it had transferred to the staff but that I had to be careful, because it could also be the death of me.

He sat beside me and said, "Matt, the staff looks on you with so much respect for what you are doing, but you run circles around everyone. Dial your efforts back to 67 percent of what you're giving now, and you'll still be out in front of us."

He continued, "As ironic as it might sound, Matt, perfectionism hampers us from being our very best."

To be honest, even with all of the success our team had experienced, I still saw areas that needed improvement. But something clicked a few days after that talk. I began examining my aim for perfection and realized that somewhere I had gotten the pursuit of perfection and the pursuit of purpose confused. I continually expected more of myself and felt I had the potential to be more successful, so I would take on projects and more obligations to provide a better product or experience. I had a hard time defining what success was for me because I put too much pressure on myself to be successful.

Looking back, I believe at that moment God began showing me that my perfectionism was the voice of the oppressor, the enemy.[5] I've come a long way since those moments. I've learned that I don't have to achieve perfection all the time. I don't have to have such elevated expectations. What I need to have is realistic expectations—goals that challenge me but don't kill me.

What I've learned about myself—and am still learning—is that no matter how beautifully crafted the stories are that I produce or to what degree I compose a shot or edit a sequence, I will likely still be able to find flaws in my own work, and so will others. I've realized that my idealism will never be sheltered from the world; other people will still be able to see that I am not perfect. As a matter of fact, people seldom expect us to be perfect, but somehow there is no way to avoid seeing our own imperfections.

POWER IN AUTHENTICITY

I used to hate the journalistic expression *story*—as in, "*War and Peace* is a good story." It seemed to me that a story was something very different from real life—something that needed a beginning, a middle, and an end—something that needed to be shaped or even invented. But as I sat there that evening with the missionary, I could easily recall the pain, the sense of a loss for words, the feeling of every eye in the place staring at me, waiting for me to screw up. As I shared this with him, I suddenly realized that my terrifying experience made for an encouraging story. God designed that meeting between the missionary and me so that we could share our stories with one another—stories that were real, raw, and needed to be told.

The true test of our story is that we be authentic and organic. That we need to learn how to turn off the inner voice that is mocking us, taunting us, and telling us our work, speech, story, photograph, or first draft cannot compare to the great works of art or the art we have yet to create. And addressing you, my fellow storytellers, I am here to tell you that your mind and your eyes are amazing gifts given to you, and no one can hear or see your story until it's told. God wants us to be ourselves and to know it's okay to be imperfect. Don't worry if your story doesn't seem to be as good as the stories of others. Storytelling requires authenticity that blossoms from the soil of your own truth.

We all can tell a story. Matter of fact, each of us does it every day, and we rarely notice. "You'll never guess who I ran into today and I bet you'll never guess what she said." "Did you hear the one about the nun, the priest, and the pastor who walked into a bar . . ." Our lives are made up of stories. We are made of stories. We all have stories inside us. They are part of our soul. They are who we are, they shape us, and they define us.

Stories affect what we do, how we feel, and who we are. Stories inspire us. Stories motivate us. Stories change us and in turn, change the world around us. When we are honest with ourselves and with others, stories help us tell our most important truths. But a story won't be able to accomplish any of these things if our fear of imperfection keeps us from sharing it. Nor will it affect anyone's life if the story is shared but never heard, because it's not enough just to share a story—someone has to take the time to stop . . . and listen.

FIVE

LISTENING

There's a lot of difference between listening and hearing.

—G. K. Chesterton

Several years ago, I started guest lecturing at a few universities and speaking regularly at workshops and conferences. When you put yourself out there like that, you usually get a lot of questions like, "How did you do that?" "Why did you do it that way?" or "How did you get that response?"

There is a lot of *how, how, why, why, why, how, how.*

When I respond to the questions, I typically get a fifty-fifty response—almost like taking a poll on who likes dogs and who likes cats. The outcome is always a draw. Some people love the answers; others seem frustrated by them. I'm not bothered by either the questions or the responses because I really enjoy helping people understand the inner workings of story. But I do feel sad for those who seem frustrated with my responses because I know some of them were looking for a magical answer, a secret key, the one step that would instantly propel their story-telling to the next level.

When you pull back the curtain and reveal The Great and Powerful Oz, there are no shiny buttons and levers, rather just ideas tumbling around in a head like socks in a dryer. But taken in its panoptic sense, the science of storytelling is all about answering the question that continuously haunts our minds: *How?*

For most, storytelling seems easy because there is not a lot of baffling subject matter like there is when you're talking philosophy and science. But when you have to describe the storytelling process, it's like trying to answer how an iPhone really works, or how bad things happen to good people or even how galaxies stretch across the vast emptiness of space.

LEARNING TO LISTEN

Recently, I presented a talk on the art of storytelling at a church conference. The room was packed. I talked about the power of an image and how to tell a story through arresting sequences. I showed a lot of stories that I've worked on, and I broke down the process of how I capture the essence of someone and get them to open up in front of my camera.

Afterward, as I was collecting my things, I began answering questions. You know, the *how, how, why, why, why, how, how.*

When someone asks me, "How can I learn to tell better stories?" my usual answer is, "Go to the masters!" (One time someone actually responded, "What does golf have to do with storytelling?") What I always mean by that is they should go to the masters of storytelling. Consume yourself with their work. Learn from them. Take apart every photo, each sequence, every caption, and analyze what they did and how they did it.

But this time I gave a different answer. I told them storytelling is personal and no matter the mode of storytelling, it really comes down to the most basic human senses, starting and ending with listening. Nothing is more personal or intimate than listening. Every story needs to have a story*teller* and a story *listener*, but even as the teller, we still have to take time to listen to the details of the story before we tell it or before we release the shutter, capturing a moment that suspends time.

Listening helps you identify the subject matter of the story.

Listening helps you feel.

Listening helps you experience the memorable.

Listening allows you to relate to people.

Listening helps to honor people's presence, and when you honor their presence, you get to their deeper, essential self.

I love the way David Ritz sums up listening in *The Writer*: "Learning to listen has been the great lesson of my life. You can't capture a subject or render someone lifelike, you can't create a living voice, with all its unique twists and turns, without listening. Now there are those who listen while waiting breathlessly to break in. For years, that was me. But I'm talking about patient listening, deep-down listening, listening with the heart as well as the head, listening in a way that lets the person know you care, that you want to hear what she has to say, that you're enjoying the sound of her voice."[1]

DISTRACTED AND DISCONNECTED

Think about the last time you fully listened to someone, the last time you fully listened to yourself. If it's been a while, don't feel bad. I'm guilty of this too.

Our culture really doesn't encourage listening. As a matter of fact, one of the reasons listening is so difficult is that the modern world seems to be organized against it. We are surrounded by endless sources of noise, we are pushed to multitask, and many of us have tuned our listening back to a quarter of what it used to be without even realizing it has happened. We've forgotten that listening is our conscious contextual navigation system. Rather we've become unconsciously aware. We check out. Disconnect. Get preoccupied. All when we're meeting with someone. Our eyes look directly into their faces while our minds are on the technology in our pockets. Or we're thinking about what we're going to say next. Or maybe we're thinking about our next project or deadline.

We are distracted.

Distracted by the subtle. Our appearances. Our possessions.

Distracted by our commitments. Our jobs. Our finances.

Distracted by fear. Our insecurities. Our futures.

The list can go on and on.

Let's face it, sometimes we *want* to be distracted. We welcome distractions in our lives because they are a great excuse to get us out of doing the difficult things that require our attention and focus. We love pretending that these minor things are so important that they take priority over the larger things in life like spending time with family, working on our life goals, or spending time with the One who created us.

But distractions are like a ravenously hungry person downing a can of Red Bull for dinner. Distractions rob us of hearing the voices around us and the Voice within us.

THE SOUNDS THAT SURROUND US

It was almost nine years into my photojournalist career. I had ping-ponged around the country and the world covering events as small as a state fair in Missouri and as life-changing as the death of Pope John Paul II. I had experienced things that had changed me deeply and internally, things known only to me, as invisible to the naked eye as the period after the Dr on a Dr Pepper can. The Matt of 2005 was significantly different than the Matt who had begun his photojournalist career in 1996.

Despite all this, when I look back, I realize I had no clue what I was doing. Whatever I was doing was working—call it dumb luck—but I would later realize there is this 1 percent margin where technique and the ability to capture a moment intersect, and I happened to fit within that very thin margin. Most of the time, I found myself dancing like Ed Grimley to keep from falling off on the other side.[2] Where I floundered was in carefully listening to my interviews and my surroundings. If you asked me then what true listening was, I would have said paying attention. I would later find out that paying attention is just the half of it.

It wasn't until I met award-winning storyteller and friend Mark Anderson that I learned what true listening was. Mark is the type of guy whose heart is two sizes too big—it's one of his best characteristics. He has these contemplative eyes, full of wisdom as a result of all the stories he has told and witnessed, yet warm with optimism and hope. And he has a Southern ease (even though he hails from Iowa) that makes him stick out in the frozen tundra of Minnesota. Mark taught me the value of listening. He taught me to listen long enough to find the humanity and the life in everything and not be a "drive-by shooter." I learned that great sound happens when you listen for great sound; it will take you to great pictures and it will take you to your story. I realized that the ultimate goal in storytelling is to tell stories in such a way that even the people who were actually there learned something more after hearing it retold.

Every morning I would venture out into the ever-changing Minnesota weather, climb into my white Ford Explorer, roll down the front windows, and follow the meandering road skirting the Louisville Swamp, Chaska Lake, and Courthouse Lake. The sun would break through the trees right at the bend of the road of Bluff Creek and Flying Cloud, and the rays would reflect off the hood of my SUV, partially blinding me for a moment. The sound a car makes while I'm driving is music to my ears; I don't know why, but I love it. I love the way the exhaust spits out a clamoring of notes as it rumbles from the engine to the tailpipe, like rolling thunder during an Oklahoma storm. One morning during my drive, my windows were down and I heard a distant, faint scream. Almost as if on cue, I veered right, pulling onto the bridge to Shakopee, and I immediately saw smoke and flames coming from St. Mark's—a Gothic church built in 1865.

I parked my car. The first fire truck was pulling on to the narrow street at the corner of Fourth and Atwood. In these types of situations, as a photographer you need to first shoot what is going to get away and then step back to focus on someone who can reveal the emotion and the enormity of the story. I was somewhere near the end of one of the dozen fire trucks, getting an artsy shot of water leaking out of the joint between hoses, when I heard, "Oh my! This is worse than when Jerry Whatever-His-Name jumped in to Nyssens Lake and had a pike bite him in the you-know-where!" in that classic Northern accent the movie *Fargo* made famous. I spun around and mic'ed this woman, because I knew in a small town there is only one thing that spreads quicker than a fire: gossip.

Margie stood on her street corner in the shadow of the steeple like a mother hen ready to roost. She began fretting. And then something happened.

Margie whipped open her flip phone—you know, the ones that look like a clamshell—and began calling everyone she knew, one by one.

Flip! "You'll never guess what happened!"

Flip! "Well, the windows are all intact, but there's a big hole in the roof!"

Flip! "You've gotta get down here!"

Let's just say it didn't take long until every person in the neighborhood knew exactly what was going on. That night, thanks to Margie and her made-for-TV personality, the city of

Minneapolis was introduced to not just another building on fire, but to a highly personal glimpse into the impact of this tragedy on a local community.

I learned that if we spend time being a conscious observer and, in this case, a conscious listener, we can capture the simplest of details. Those details are the juice, the essence of the story, what moves an audience and stirs their souls. And the grandness of life is made up of the small moments we listen for.

GOD AND MY GPS

Listening is one of the hardest things we face in our present world. It's also the hardest thing to do when trying to hear God's voice.

There are a lot of times I fight to hear the faint whisper. For me, God seems to talk only when something is about to happen, as I was reminded recently on a trip to the beach with my family.

It was our family's last trip before summer's close. We were driving to the beach, and traveling for us can be a little intense at times. My wife is admittedly directionally challenged, and though I have a good sense of polar north, I also like to engage in conversation in the car and sometimes get distracted when we're on a great topic. Between the two of us, we usually make a few wrong left turns, but they eventually become right with a little help. Needless to say, most of the time we have on our GPS (Tom Tom), which our kids have affectionately named "Tomasita."

During this particular trip we were somewhere on I-45 in Houston and distracted by the skyline when Tomasita began talking. She was telling us to "turn around at the next available opportunity." I think we finally heard the GPS after both of our kids hollered in exasperation, "Turn around!"

As we recalibrated, my daughter asked, "Daddy, why weren't you listening to Tomasita? She was telling you where to go!"

I think I gave the excuse of "we were looking at the city and talking," which we were. But as I chewed on her question a little bit more, I realized again it's hard for us to listen because of the things that pervade our attention. And if we have a hard time listening to the audible GPS command directions, no wonder we're having a hard time listening to God.

On the highway of life, God is telling us a story. A story of our lives. A narrative he has written for us. A story about his will for us in this world. We find it hard to listen for that story because on the highway of life, God is like that GPS in my car. The deal is, he is the only one that knows the right paths we should take, but we're so preoccupied with the small, unimportant stuff—we're tuned out, looking at the city and jamming to the radio, too busy to be bothered. Meanwhile, he always has to say, in some shape or form, "Take a left here. Keep right and exit in three miles." It always seems God is there just when you need him, "You've missed your turn. Make a U-turn at the next available opportunity." And just like the kids in the backseat, sometimes he sends a gong and clashing symbol to get our attention: "Where on earth are you going?"

LOOKING BENEATH THE SURFACE

At times we find ourselves in a spiritual crisis, and in those moments God is speaking to us amid all the confusion of our lives, against all our comprehension and controlling . . . but we don't hear him. Christ is making an appeal that disrupts the way we think and know and believe . . . but it disturbs us, so we tune him out.

God wants us to be story listeners. He wants us to listen to *our* story and to *his* story. That means digging deeper and getting to the core of the story God is telling. On the surface the narratives are those we initially see, like the guy who seems to have it all together—unbelievable job, a great family, volunteering at his church and in his community, always flashing his signature winning grin. Or maybe it's the woman whose house is always perfect, who works full-time and is still actively involved in her children's school, who runs a locally recognized blog in her spare time, and who always looks like she walked straight off a magazine cover.

However, the further you dig and the deeper you go—as you find your way beneath the surface level of their visual depiction—you find the hidden meaning, a deeper meaning, a more extensive message often buried far below the outward appearance, just like the underwater world in Jules Verne's *Twenty Thousand Leagues Under the Sea*. What you find is the rest of the story. A story of truth, longing, despair, loss, fear, or uncertainty, and the list could go on and on.

In many ways we have poisoned our stories. We only share what we see rather than what we have learned through listening. We are demoralized—unresponsive to the gift of listening for more. We are not fully aware of our stories and those we are telling; they are half-truths.

Most women I know secretly (or not-so-secretly) despise

the "Proverbs 31 woman" depicted in the last chapter of the book of Proverbs. This chapter consists of the sayings of a mother passed down to her son, encouraging him to look for a wife with good character. The description is meant to guide and inspire, but for so many women it feels suffocating and overwhelming. King Lemuel's mother paints the picture of a flawless woman who excels at everything she puts her hand to. And the image of this woman suddenly becomes an impossible standard in many women's minds that they somehow feel they have to live up to.

But we often fail to realize that we're reading this woman's résumé. We're seeing her at her best, with the lighting just perfect, on a day when things are going so well it feels almost magical. I wonder, if this woman truly were to exist, what her flaws would have been? What would her underlying story have been? If I took a camera into her home and filmed her story, what would I discover about what she's been through, how her struggles and failures have shaped her, and what she hopes for beyond all else?

There are always stories we *don't* see hidden beneath the story we do see.

THE WONDER OF A CHILD

Sometimes we lose the impact of a story because we've heard it or read it so many times. As a child, we would watch our favorite movie or read our favorite story over and over until we drove our parents crazy. As we get older, we crave variety and freshness and easily become bored with the familiar. We want what's new, what's hot off the press, what no one else has seen yet.

But there is wisdom to be found in the past, knowledge to be discovered from those who have gone before us, and value in savoring a story rather than racing through it.

Do you ever find yourself tired of the stories and messages found in God's Word? If so, you're not alone. There are a lot of times when I read the Bible and sit back and scratch my head in bewilderment. For example, anytime I try to read the book of Numbers I feel like I'm back in history class. Reading Numbers for me is like watching paint dry. There, I said it. It's one of those books where you need to pay attention to every single word in hopes that it will finally make sense. The text is hard to take in, almost like wading through a molasses swamp on a cold day in February.

But what intrigues me about this book is that it's a story about God and his relationship with his people. I know there's good stuff in there—even relevant stuff, like why do people blatantly disrespect God when he demands obedience? How does faith get passed down from one generation to the next? Or how about this: in a world where everything is competing for our attention and where we are faced with temptations, how do we define ourselves yet keep true to our calling and mission? We know that God wrote *all* Scripture with *all* of us in mind. When we take the time to dig deeper into the story, we can discover not only what God meant to communicate to the Israelites of the Old Testament but also what he wants to reveal about himself to us through the text today.

We've become so accustomed to God's Word and his story that at times we let it have little value in our lives. When is the last time you celebrated the incredible gift of your salvation? So often we are bored by it—uninterested and apathetic toward the story that changed the destiny of all of mankind.

It's sad, when you think about it—we have so much at our fingertips, yet we often look past it. We're tempted by the material things of this world and the people in it. We focus on the landscape and tune out the navigator. Our distractions plague us. We interrupt our narratives. We let the distractions in our lives rewrite our stories.

But when we look at a child we see a freshness. An openness. An untainted view of the world. An undistracted wonderment toward everything. Their eyes and ears are wide open to fully immerse themselves in the now, enjoying the moment at hand. Growing up, my kids were constantly asking us why and how. Children have a deep desire to absorb everything around them. They listen contently and have a drive to explore. A passion to learn. An innate sense to dig deeper. They're full of questions and wait eagerly to hear what we will say next.

The art of listening is fundamental to our growth as storytellers and as Christians. Being a storyteller and a Christian is about having the wonderment of a child—being able to listen with a sense of awe, not worried about what comes next or who might be watching us. Just intently listening.

LIFE IS IN THE DETAILS

Photographers and storytellers are aware of the details of the stories they are telling. They keenly observe the intimate details of a picture or the eloquent phrasing of a sentence, because these small details reveal the DNA or the nuclei that bring a story to life. They will wait patiently for the right moment by listening to their surroundings or the subtle contexts within their viewfinder, all in the effort to capture a photo that uncovers a powerful visual statement. As much as this sounds like an oxymoron (and if you have ever met a creative person, you may argue this point), creatives live in the details—they really do. They listen to the canvas to determine which way the paintbrush should move. They pay attention to the purpose behind the story they're trying to tell. They take notes of the finer points that will make up their final creation. They unearth deeper truths by visually listening.

Listening is also at the core of our Christian experience and can be summed up in this profound passage in Scripture: "Anyone who answers without listening is foolish and confused."[3] As the pages turn on the greatest story ever told, it provides commentary on the pitfalls of turning a deaf ear to God's Word: "Don't stop listening to correction, my child, or you will forget what you have already learned."[4] Failure to listen to wise words only diminishes the person who ignores them.

Learning to listen is as essential to becoming a great storyteller and story listener as it is to developing a great relationship with God. It's all about listening. Unless you truly focus and pay attention to the story, you won't be able to identify the subject matter or how you felt as you viewed an image or heard a story, let alone the impressions you walked away with. Concentrating on the story helps you discern what aspects of the telling itself—such as the teller's voice, tone, style, or the message the image or scene is trying to convey—helped make the listening experience memorable.

Finally, it's about the details. God is in the details of a story. The nooks and crannies. The gaps. The subtle nuances within the image. The spaces between the words and intonation. The subtle points that are often missed. Being attentive to the details helps add context to the circumstances relating to the time, place, or situation, which all add to the story's impact.

As I've grown as a storyteller and a Christian, I have come to rely on intently listening to my subjects, to myself, and to God. The Bible speaks volumes about the value of listening and how we should "be willing to listen and slow to speak."[5] Listening is hard when the modern world is organized against it. We need to change our mind-set in order to change our attitude. Simply put, we need to adjust and focus on someone other than ourselves and our own distractions, and by doing so we will create something that is more meaningful.

By being observant and really listening to what's going on in our lives and in the lives of those around us, we are able to tell a more meaningful story—one that is authentic and that captures the whole picture. Otherwise, if we choose to be ignorant and disregard the deeper and truer image we should project, this reveals we are not fully listening. We need to look below the superficial narrative of our lives and find deeper meaning in what may appear simple on the surface.

The gospel of Luke tells the tale of two sisters, Martha and Mary. The sisters welcomed Jesus as a guest into their home. And as we all know, when you have guests over, you should offer them something to eat or drink, which is what Martha immediately set herself to doing. But somewhere along the line Martha became openly upset with her sister because Mary had decided to listen to Jesus rather than help her prepare the food. Jesus shocked Martha by openly lauding Mary's desire to hear the Word of God, telling her, "Martha, Martha, you are worried and upset about many things. Only one thing is important. Mary has chosen the better thing, and it will never be taken away from her."[6]

We can also see this narrative nudge for attention in the Old Testament with an interaction between Samuel and God that really hits the point home. God is standing before Samuel when he calls Samuel using an audible voice. We can easily imagine Samuel standing there, eager to perform God's will as he answers, "Speak, LORD. I am your servant and I am listening."[7]

God's desire for us is to recognize that he is present in our everyday lives, no matter how much strife, division, desperation, and failure surrounds us.

Paul writes, "I always thank my God for you because of the grace God has given you in Christ Jesus. I thank God because in Christ you have been made rich in every way, in all your speaking and in all your knowledge. Just as our witness about Christ has been guaranteed to you, so you have every gift from God while you wait for our Lord Jesus Christ to come again. Jesus will keep you strong until the end so that there will be no wrong in you on the day our Lord Jesus Christ comes again. God, who has called you into fellowship with his Son, Jesus Christ our Lord, is faithful."[8]

We are encouraged to listen closely to what God is saying in the din of our lives. As storytellers we must be attentive, concentrating on the literal and figurative details of the stories we're charged with telling. We are to be consumed with those around us—not distracted. To be focused in the here and the now. To live in the moment.

PART 2

CAPTURE

SIX

MOMENT

There is only one time that is important—NOW! It is the
most important time because it is the only time that we
have any power.

—LEO TOLSTOY

I have this infatuation with aesthetics. It's more like a love
affair with how things look. You know, the art of the beautiful. The ugly. The sublime. The comic. The serene. They
are the things that spike the interest of our senses or the emotional values that are sometimes called taste. I have a hard time
shutting it off. I think in pictures and in images. I see things in
an eight-by-ten frame. My mind is a mental camera. My eyes
have become viewfinders.

Even more so, I have a veneration for moments. The lim-
inal space that links one instance to another. These moments

are strung together, not haphazardly but carefully woven into the tapestry of life. We see these moments as evanescent. Almost out of sight. Lost in the fabric of each minute, hour, day, and year. They are fleeting glimpses that to many look like ordinary consequences, but are actually extraordinary glimpses into our human experience and our world.

To put it simply, I look for aesthetic moments. Decisive moments. The golden moments of our lives.

Robert Frost says, "A poem begins with a lump in the throat,"[1] and stories are no different. Those lumps are moments, and stories need moments. Tangible moments that communicate fear, love, sadness, and, above all else, hope. These points in time are intriguing to me,[2] because as a storyteller, I always want to know more. I want to dig deeper. To find the meaning and beauty in everything. But capturing a moment is more than pointing a camera or filling in the margins of a notebook. It's about the decisive moments: "A simultaneous recognition, in a fraction of a second, of the significance of an event as well as the precise organization of forms which gives that event its proper expression."[3] It's when the timing is just right for the storyteller—when the photographer clicks the shutter and captures an amazing image that reveals the seene in a way that helps tell a story in a compelling way.

CHASING SUNSETS

Chasing sunsets is a saying I've adopted over the years to describe the times when passion collides with life, and everything else is muffled because you're focused on the beauty of the moment.

During these times, life is at its zenith; there is clarity. These are the moments we experience something so powerful, so intense, so beautiful, that our soul snaps an internal picture, forever engraving in our memory what it was that suddenly focused our attention, grabbed our hearts, and made us think. I like the descriptive image of sunsets, because there's something that happens in the waning hours of the day that causes all of us to look toward the horizon, breathe, and reflect. Sunsets are life's way of reminding us to focus for a second.

There is something magical about twilight. (Just to clarify, I'm *not* talking about a certain book series that threatened to ruin the beauty of this word.) Twilight is the brief period in the evening that appears between the shift of one segment of time to another—from light to dark. In the morning when the shift is made from dark to light, this reverse transition is called dawn. There is such intense yet peaceful beauty in the moments during which our world awakens and slips into slumber each day. They bring to mind thoughts of other transitions in our lives. Prearranged markers. Ceremonies of significance. Rites of passage.

Sailors look to the horizon for guidance. They live by the old adage, "Red sky at night, sailor's delight. Red sky at morning, sailor's warning."[4] At the transitions of each day, they look to the sky with anticipation to decipher its appearance—the color, the form of the atmosphere, the direction of the wind, and the type of the clouds—all to predict the upcoming weather.

For photographers, there is something magical about the gloaming; the sunlight during that time has a soft, warm hue. For a few glorious moments, the sun illuminates buildings and landscapes with a red and orange tincture. The subtle, warm tones make practically anything look good. The "golden hour" of our lives is made up of the moments in life that reveal people at their best and worst. Entwined in those ordinary moments is the extraordinary.

A RARE FIND

Regardless of the medium, storytelling is about finding moments—catching glimpses—and using them to foreshadow as we carefully place them one by one throughout our stories, like a trail of coins that finally leads us to the treasure. Without a moment there is no story. Storytellers work hard to seize that moment. They know if you wait too long for the perfect moment it will pass you by. It's realizing when to trust one's instincts and knowing when to surrender the quest of perfectionism to the plausible.

Finding those moments is hard work. It means getting close to the story we're trying to tell. Getting to know our subjects. Building a connection that will pull us closer to understanding who they really are. The storyteller's process is to size up a situation, subject, and story by watching and anticipating how the action and expression will unfold.

A storyteller's job is not to be a hunter searching for prey, but rather to tell the story that might not otherwise be told. The more you let your heart engage with the story, the more your audience will connect with the story.

However, there is pain in the process. Pain in waiting, listening, and holding on for the right moment. Pain in that moment when action, reaction, gesture, and quote reveal a deeper level of recognition, discovery, and feeling.

The precise arrangement of forms, artistic composition, and narrative are what make the moment powerful. *Capture. Sketch. Record. Write. Jot.* Archive the memorable. Learn to identify those moments and recognize what they look like. Patience is a must; time is your friend and not your keeper. You need to be spontaneous and incredibly meticulous, refined and highly disciplined. The process itself is enjoyable so cherish it, because it, too, will expire.

One of the most challenging stories I ever had the privilege of telling was a rare find. You know, one of those stories you cannot believe hasn't been told yet. Nestled among the ten thousand lakes and northern wilderness of Minnesota is a one-of-a-kind summer camp. The camp is a fully immersed camping experience for individuals with Down syndrome.

A number of years ago, I spent several days hanging out with the staff and kids, building relationships and enjoying their company. Through the experience I met thirteen-year-old Katie, a bundle of energy, a social butterfly, and the center of the camp's attention.

What is so special about this story is that Katie had just found out, by piecing things together, that she was different. Her parents hadn't told her up until that point that she had Down syndrome because they had wanted her to have a normal childhood and feel like a typical kid. But in reality, she was far from typical. She was unique; she was special; she was Katie.

Katie and I became friends during my time spent shadowing her with my camera. I was able to witness firsthand some of her struggles and her successes. In many ways, she was no different than any other teenager. She thought her mom wasn't cool, she swooned over Leonardo DiCaprio, and she obsessed over her hair in front of the mirror.

I remember asking her how she felt about being different. Timidly she answered with her head hung low, "I hate it!" You could hear a pin drop right after she said that. But after a few seconds passed, she lifted her head high, smiled, and said, ". . . but I love it anyway!" What Katie hinted at in that moment was that she embraced her uniqueness. Yes, it was difficult at times, but overall she celebrated being different. So what if her life wasn't within the parameters that others set for "normal"? Who is normal these days anyway?

Everyone knows that at summer camp, every kid away from the boundaries of home ends up with a crush on someone by the week's end. This camp was no different. As if on cue, just as the sun began to set and twilight appeared, I heard a giggle from among the campers sitting around the campfire. There, right in front of my lens like magic, I saw Katie get her first kiss from a boy named Trent. He then held her gently, looking into her eyes as he rubbed her back for a moment before a camp counselor ran over to separate them as Katie giggled and repeated over and over, "He likes me."

CAPTURING THE UNORDINARY

Moments like this are ephemeral. They are a brief look into life. They are ordinary moments that reveal a great deal more than the milestones of our lives. If we could just stop ourselves from trying to capture the perfect moment, we might actually find true and real moments subtly living in the in-between. If we resist our temptation to attain perfection, we might find the real moments. Something more than just the milestones of life. More than those crucial stages in our existence. There is more than just life and death. Our lives are held together by many quieter moments: the moment you meet the love of your life, the moment you realize your parents are not perfect, the moment you say a final good-bye to a loved one, the moment your child grasps your face with her chubby fingers and says, "You're my best daddy," the moment you finally choose forgiveness over hate. No matter how big or small the moment is, it touches your life in an incalculable way.

Sunsets are inevitable. Each day ends with one. That's the way it's been since God said, "Let there be light," and he separated the light from the darkness, calling the light "day" and the darkness "night."[5] Yet most of us pay little or no attention to this ordinary occurrence that is an extraordinary moment in our day, life, and world. Ordinary moments are the pages in our life's story. But the reality is, there is nothing ordinary about our lives.

My work has taken me all over the world and has put me in many historical moments over the last decade and a half—moments I will never forget for as long as I live. But I can also tell you many of the moments that impacted me the most were the ones I never expected.

It was 2005 and the cobblestone-lined streets of Rome were barely lit by the sun as it set behind the stone plaza of St. Peter's Square. Just after dusk, the narrow entryways into the square became clogged with people gathering as the bells of St. Peter's

Basilica tolled, signaling the papal apartment had been sealed off. Mourners fell to their knees in grief. Standing in St. Peter's Square, you could not help but turn your eyes to the heavens. At his death on April 2, 2005, with thousands packed into the piazza and a group of doctors, nuns, priests, and bishops by his bedside, John Paul's papacy ended.

You also could not help but hear the prayers that saturated the Vatican and the area surrounding it—prayers for the passing of the pope and hope for the future of the church as millions of grief-stricken Roman Catholics personally began paying their respects. I remember it was hard at times to concentrate between the waves of silence, cheers, and shock. I had covered thousands of news stories in my career, but nothing as powerful, honoring, and poignant. There were the sounds of reverence, when one could hear the clatter of rosary beads and whispered prayers. In all of the events I have covered, never have I seen a crowd this large and this respectful. In a way, the peace, tranquility, and humility seemed fitting for a man whom some considered a contemporary saint.

Late that night, I was invited to view Pope John Paul with Cardinal McCarrick, the Archbishop Emeritus of Washington, and pay my respects. I stood there beneath the canopy of Bernini's altar surrounded by the golden domes and Michelangelo's *Pietà*— and in the middle of all of that beauty lay a man filled with humility, beloved by so many. In a faith tradition filled with icons, the pope is the living symbol of unity for the Catholic Church. With the Swiss Guard in striped pantaloons flanking my right and left in rigid vigil, I stood by the pontiff in silence and prayer.

As a Christian for many years, I've noticed that God's people are often more taken up with working for him rather than with worshipping him. But that day I saw something utterly opposite. As I left the viewing, I saw something hidden away from the cameras and the world. I saw something so holy, something so emotional, along the sides of the basilica: groups of nuns and priests lined the altars, kneeling and praying. I could not help but notice one woman outstretched on the Italian marble floor facing the heavens, openly weeping. At that precise second, I felt my presence not only as an observer to history but as a journalist, and I stood in awe and in deep recognition of how privileged I was to be there, experiencing such a sacred moment. I soaked in the enormity of the moment. The scale of the story. This had been just another assignment. Just another story in the ordinary life of a photojournalist. Yet there was nothing ordinary about what I experienced.

But the story doesn't end there. On my return trip to the States, after all the pomp and circumstance, the sea of cassock robes and zucchettos, and the papal inauguration of Pope Benedict XVI . . . sitting there on American Flight 111 in seat 10J reflecting on the last month's work, something happened to me.

Looking out the window at an evening sky that burned orange toward the horizon, I felt a nudge to do more with my life. I experienced a moment of clarity where things in my life began to come into sharper focus. I sat there perplexed, unsure how to make the next step; I was full of doubt. I remember pleading with God to show me a sign. To show me that beyond a shadow of a doubt, I needed to drop everything I was doing and take a road less traveled.

Just then I opened my pocket Bible and began to read the story about Jesus being tested by the Pharisees and Sadducees. They were pleading with him to show them a sign, and Jesus replied, "When evening comes, you say, 'It will be fair weather, for the sky is red.' And in the morning, 'Today it will be stormy, for the sky is red and overcast.'"[6]

It was a moment that communicated volumes to me. God suddenly began stirring my soul. What I had just read transcended time and situation to show me that my sin was not in asking God for a sign but in my reason for asking. I hadn't really been searching for guidance as much as I had been looking for proof, just as the Pharisees of old had. Didn't I trust him more than that?

In that moment, I knew God had placed a call on my life to use my talents to help his kingdom. I didn't know what that looked like or how to go about making something like that happen; my life to that point had been spent in broadcast news and sitting in a pew on Sunday mornings. But God had a plan. God had his timing.

HOLY INTERSECTIONS

God wants us to have these kinds of decisive moments with him. To wait in solace. To wait in faith. To wait with hope. To wait in prayer. All so that we may have a moment of understanding. A moment when God barges into our lives, leaving us with no question that he is there, that there is a purpose and plan for each of us, and we'll never be the same because of the encounter. God crafts these divine moments specifically for each of us. They are priceless opportunities to actively engage in his plan. They are his challenge. His nudge to move us from the mundane to the miraculous.

The Bible is riddled with intersections where challenges and divine moments collide, but there is one in particular that really hits home for me.

Moses' life was chock-full of divine collisions. He wrote, "[Lord], teach us to number our days, that we may gain a heart of wisdom."[7] This is from a man whose life had been spent waiting for the right moments. Forty years in exile. The burning bush. Crossing the Red Sea, then traversing the wilderness more than over one million followers. The blessing of food and water in the midst of the dangers of the desert. And then the Ten Commandments. God blessed Moses with a lifetime of moments.

Moses realized that every season of life had a different message and story from God revealing a divine purpose. He recognized the value of every day we have on earth. He realized the moment he was in. He realized God's promise. He appreciated what mattered. He realized the season he was given and that never before had the destinies of so many been determined by the choices of so few. He was awakened to the power of a moment. He became cognizant of the moments God puts before us—those teaching opportunities that shape our lives and faith.

Moses teaches us that we should be alert to the divine moments God has for us. We spend our lives collecting things rather than the moments God has planned. The challenge? Waiting. Going through life with its routines and expectations and being able to look for the divine moments when they come along.

Moments, like sunsets, are each different—unique and beautiful seconds captured in time. We can't plan them. They are moments created for us by One who loves us. They are moments we need to strive to be ready for and to take advantage of when the miraculous happens in the ordinary.

Everything in life is part of a great story: your story. But a moment has the ability to communicate so much: fear, love, sadness, and, above all else, hope. The potential of a single moment has a way of transforming itself into action—but we have to patiently wait for that moment. For that instant when everything suddenly comes into focus. That moment is one worth waiting for.

SEVEN

PERSPECTIVE

I never ask God to give me anything; I only ask him to put me where things are.

—MEXICAN PROVERB

Photographers work in the realm of reality. Their eye and their camera are one, though the camera captures what the eye rarely sees. It pushes past what is seen, capturing a dynamic range of light, color, and spatial orientation that the eye cannot comprehend. These ingredients help form perspective for the audience. You can compare it to the way a writer uses the element of foreshadowing or a painter uses texture and shading to add depth and meaning. As artists, we use our tools to see into the soul of the scene we are trying to recreate. We are burdened to impart emotion, depth, and context into our work and make it our responsibility to transport time and place from half a world away to our viewer's living room, gallery, or electronic screen. We see the world selectively through our viewfinder or our own place in the world, but we seek to bring meaning through our craft and works. We want to enlighten. We attempt to reveal more of the story—a more arresting view of the world we live in opposed to the one-dimensional veil of concrete, electronic devices, and status updates that hold our attention. We hope to edify.

Maybe it's because I'm a photographer or maybe it's because it's in my DNA, but I'm constantly looking for perspective in everything, from the unique Shoe House off of Route 30 near where I grew up in York, Pennsylvania, to the subjects of my work and the stories they're telling.

Perspective gives us meaning. It frames our world, gives us a point of reference, and allows us to see different possibilities. Perspective and its genetic code are made up of the combination of *what* you are looking *at* with *where* you are looking *from*. *What* you are listening *to* and *where* you are listening *from*. Perspective fuels how we act and even what we think and how we feel. It allows us to see the extraordinary in the ordinary. It brings focus to the bizarre elements of society. Perspective shows that people often behave in strange ways and common sense is the best guide to discerning human behavior. Perspective allows us to begin to understand the complex and to shape our lives.

Think about the last time you looked at an image, watched a movie, or gazed at a sunset. Your eye is really only drawn to one part of the image—not the whole thing. If you don't believe me, stop reading this book for a second and look up around you for a picture or piece of artwork. Now notice how one thing or element in the image catches your eye more than the rest.

The way you're viewing that image is called perspective, and it's one of the techniques used in photography to help tell a story in a single picture or a progression of images. Have you ever sat in a window seat on an airplane and looked out below at the city skyline or the patchwork of fields? From thirty thousand feet in the air, you were visually experiencing them as if they were presented on a grand stage. Things come into focus . . . like the hedges that run along the road now become property lines for bordering farms. The farms become a patchwork quilt that comforts the earth, and the streams turn into details that break the monotony. Perspective adds impact, depth, and life because of the tie between the subject and scene in terms of distance, space, and scale. This gives us the illusion that we're not just looking at a flat, hollowed-out object but rather something that actually has form. Something that has life. Stories are nothing without perspective. Perspective helps us understand differnt viewpoints and provides a frame of reference, opinions, beliefs, and experiences.

Storytellers look for more. They develop perspective. Connect the seemingly unconnected. Find what has been overlooked. Ask the *why* question a lot to get that thirty-thousand-foot view. They look at the architecture—the texture and character that make up the story—to really get a sense of where one fits in the world. But if you look even closer at the details of a story, you can find something romantic, something exciting, or something you can't wrap your mind around, like a Trekkie at a *Star Trek* convention.

I didn't always think or sound this way, or even look for this type of viewpoint in the ordinary. Finding perspective in my stories was something I struggled with. At the end of the day, I really didn't care about finding perspective; I was just a photo-journalist wanting to tell stories.

When young journalists first begin chasing unfolding headlines that riddle the newsstands and congest channels of twenty-four-hour news coverage, they often expect to be drowning in hundreds of good stories each day. After all, it's a big, important world. There should be a story around every corner, right? Unfortunately, even in a profession devoted to chasing good stories, many days finding a tale that penetrates expected human routines can feel like trying to find one lone endangered animal wandering in the Sahara.

Things that seemed so important—presidential motorcades, dressed-up press stages, bodyguards, and entourages—start to take on a certain predictable monotony. So even when you land in the middle of the action and you and the rest of the press pool speed after your police escort in a Ford Econovan, it can be easy to get lost in the blur.

After a little while on the circuit, you start to feel like if you've seen one politician, you've seen every politician who ever existed. They have similar ways of dressing, of making calcu-lated eye contact, of schmoozing and gesturing and massaging their audiences. As a result, journalists like me sometimes walk away feeling like they've just experienced a cross between mas-sive déjà vu and the movie *Groundhog Day*.[1]

But every once in a while, a *real* story emerges that cuts through the press conference norms and connects humans to one another. A story that captures your attention and changes your perspective.

"NICE TO MEET YOU, NICE-LEE"

During the run-up to the 2000 presidential campaign, I was locked into routine press coverage of George W. Bush's campaign stop in Harrisburg, Pennsylvania. After the regular pomp, the ceremonial hand-shaking, autographs, and photo ops, members of the press were granted brief one-on-one time with the candidate—a practice that is standard in the industry. During one of these more intimate interviews with George W. Bush, however, something certainly beyond "standard" pulled me from the sidelines into the story.

While being questioned, President Bush playfully took the microphone out of my fellow reporter's hand and started asking us both questions as if we had switched roles with him. It was an appreciated moment of humor in all the humdrum, which *might've* left a slight impression on me, even if the next parts hadn't happened.

Right after his mock interviews of us, President Bush pulled the microphone close to his chin and asked his final question. Locking his eyes onto me, he inquired simply, "What's your name?"

"Matt Knisely," I replied.

Nodding attentively, a slight smirk crept to his face as he delivered his trademark confused look made famous by Will Farrell on *Saturday Night Live*.

I knew what was coming. Wait for it . . . wait for it . . . "Nice to meet you, Nice-Lee." (This is something I've heard a million and one times in my life.)

As I left, I was struck by the way President Bush had intentionally worked to create a moment of familiarity inside of his campaign tour, but I knew it was still formulaic, the product of social graces he used with the many people he encountered.

At this point, this was a refreshing interaction but still not a story that impacted me on a deep, personal level.

The day I got pulled into the story of who President George W. Bush is and what he was doing in the world didn't occur until two and a half years later when I was working in Arizona, covering a private fund-raiser and dinner for a Gubernatorial Candidate, shortly following a national crisis. I was working in the press pool, lost in a sea of cameras and microphones and notes, listening to the president stump for a candidate, and defend the details of the United States' recent troop deployment into Afghanistan.

Everything was exactly as it always was as President Bush left the stage, sliding down the outside perimeter of the crowd of reporters. I saw his profile as he passed, striding next to me, with me in his peripheral vision. That's when he paused, pointed at me, and said, "Nice to meet you, Nice-Lee," as he continued his path outside the room and back into the expected protocol.

I was stunned. How did he do that? How did he remember me? He had to have remembered our interaction and my story.

For the media outlets, that story was about a candidate's campaign and the movement of US troops, but for me (the photographer who meets—but is never remembered by—famous, influential people), it became a story of connecting as humans.

In that moment I began to realize a simple truth about humans: a story is the shortest distance between two people, and some of the most beautiful parts of a story are best captured in isolation—in two-dimensional perspective.

The people who are remembered in life are the people who

pull you into a story—the people who add fresh perspective, angles, and points of view to the stories of our lives. The stories that penetrate life's routines are the stories that connect humans to each other. And the new perspective that is revealed helps us make sense of the world around us.

HE KNOWS US BY NAME

I shared the story about George W. with you because it reminds me of my relationship with God. It took me a while to understand I am on a first-name basis with God. That he actually cares about me as an individual. That it matters to him how I feel and what I think. The interaction I had with President Bush also showed me that there are people we view as important or "too big" who do care about those of us who view themselves as small. The interaction further revealed that God cares about our perspective. He wants us to step back. Look around. Get the bigger picture. To have our eyes wide open. He *doesn't* want us to shuffle along, eyes to the ground, distracted with the things right in front of us. Rather, he wants us to look up and be alert to what he is doing among his people in this world he has created for us. He wants us to see things from his perspective.[2]

We have a hard time trying to comprehend the fact God really cares about what we're going through. Why would someone so big care for someone so small? In a world filled with problems, plagues, and plights, sometimes it seems like God doesn't care. To many, it feels like he's too grandiose for our problems and struggles because they are so small in comparison to him.

If you're a parent or have ever taught a group of children,

then you know that kids always seem to be freaking out about something. When they're very young, it's "She hit me!" or "He said I'm a poopy-head!" A few years later it turns into the drama of best-friend betrayals and panic at forgetting to turn in the field trip permission slip. Sometimes to us, as adults, the problems of children can seem so trivial. We may think (or maybe have said aloud), "I'm sorry your friends wouldn't play with you today . . . but c'mon—do *you* have to figure out how to pay the mortgage? It's not that big of a deal. You'll get over it and make new friends."

Catherine Wallace writes, "Listen earnestly to anything your children want to tell you, no matter what. If you don't listen eagerly to the little stuff when they are little, they won't tell you the big stuff when they are big, because to them all of it has always been big stuff."[3] Some of the best parents I know are the ones who can empathize with their children and remember what it felt like to be their age. They don't talk down to their kids; they affirm what their children are thinking and let them know they understand and they care.

What I love about God is that he entered into our world so that he could experience life as we experience it. He doesn't trivialize our issues (which obviously pale in light of him and his greatness), but instead he says, "I understand. I'm here for you. And I want to help you."

Perhaps you've imagined God as a high and lofty political figure with no time for you. Perhaps you've seen him as a successful businessman whose agenda is far too filled with other, more important things. Perhaps you've seen him as a parent who just doesn't understand.

Change your perspective. See God with fresh eyes. Because

the fact is, God does care about the smallest of our problems. He knows us by name. Matthew points out that God cares about the tiny sparrow when it falls and that we're worth more than a whole flock.[4] His care and concern fill the pages and stories of the Bible.

GOD'S PERSPECTIVE

There is a story in the Gospels that really adds perspective to how much God cares about people. The story is about a group of social outcasts who were driven out of town. It's a story about how people were revolted by the way certain people looked, terrified by their differences, horrified at the thought of coming in contact with them and possibly contracting their disease. It's a story of Jesus cleansing a group of lepers.[5]

What's so incredible to me about this story is that when Jesus visited the lepers, he could've merely spoken and they would have been healed; but Jesus chose to heal them by touching them. Remember, lepers were people who were *never* approached, much less touched. They were most likely starving for physical affection, and a touch that might have seemed merely kind to us would have spoken volumes of love to them. Jesus touched the untouchables, the rejected, the castaways. The intimacy of our God is astounding yet oh so personal.

But the reality is, no matter how many stories we read or hear, we still can end up with a narrow focus. Caught up and consumed by what we have to do day in and day out. We have a sharp view of our lives and what we want to achieve. We concentrate on the things of this world rather than on things that have eternal value. We invest our time in school, jobs, status updates, blog posts, to-do lists, investments, and side jobs. Growing our reach in this world. Evolving our status in society. Germinating our portfolio. We don't often take the time to stop and view the world and the people in it from God's perspective.

I'm as guilty as the next guy. I fall prey to the same temptations. So I sit back on occasion and ponder the delicate chess moves of my life, examining them in light of God's Word, God's will, and God's warmth.

Not long ago, I was having one of these reflective times alone with God when I came across what Paul says in Romans, chapters 9 through 11. The context of these chapters is that Gentile Christians were apparently becoming arrogant about their faith in Christ. As citizens of a powerful empire, Romans, in general, looked down on Jews and the rest of the people groups that Rome had conquered. Though some of them had received the truth of the gospel, unfortunately their arrogance didn't disappear but instead changed angles. The Roman Christians began to look down upon Jews who had not yet recognized Jesus as the Messiah and Son of God, and they became arrogant about their faith. But in these chapters, Paul points to God's righteousness and his mysterious plan for saving Israel. He carefully describes God's salvation to his Roman brothers, revealing to them that God has a plan and a perspective that they are not yet aware of.

Paul says this mystery is complicated, hard to comprehend, and easy to misinterpret: even though the Jews made themselves enemies of God, his love for them is eternal. Paul further communicated how much God loves the nation of Israel: "I want you to understand this secret . . . so you will understand that you do not know everything: Part of Israel has been made stubborn, but that will change when many who are not Jews have come to God. And that is how all Israel will be saved. It is written in the Scriptures: 'The Savior will come from Jerusalem; he will take away all evil from the family of Jacob.'"[6] He clarified, "The Jews refuse to accept the Good News, so they are God's enemies. This has happened to help you who are not Jews. But the Jews are still God's chosen people, and he loves them very much because of the promises he made to their ancestors."[7] Neither the Roman Christians (in their arrogance) nor the Jews (in their narrow understanding of what the Messiah should look like) understood God's perspective. They were both missing the big picture.

God's perspective is that we find his will for us. That we look more. Open our eyes wider. Focus. Find coherency. Uncover meaning and display a sense of wonderment in the story he has written. Perspective is more than just a voice, more than just a story structure. Rather, it's about evaluating an experience— picking up on what stories have to say and measuring their impact on our lives and the life change they bestow.

Daniel Taylor writes, "Finding myself is less a matter of uncovering some supposedly pristine and genuine self within, one uncorrupted by outside influences, than it is discovering my role in various stories in which I am one of many characters. Being one character out of many in a larger story does not diminish me; it enlarges me and my possible significance. I am not an isolated individual desperately searching for illusory self and plaintively insisting on my needs and rights; rather I am a character in a story with other characters, making choices together that give our lives meaning."[8]

Perspective is about seeing a broader view and capturing our place in the world. It's about revealing the extraordinary

in the familiar . . . discovering our true purpose by looking
through a longer lens . . . uncovering the human . . . unearthing
the humane . . . exposing our true purpose. Perspective helps
us move away from a simplistic, one-dimensional view of life
and allows us to explore the depth found in our subjects—even
when the subjects are ourselves.

EIGHT

SUBJECT

*Use what talents you possess: the woods would be very
silent if no birds sang there except those that sang best.*

—Henry van Dyke

When you look at a photograph, what is the first
thing your eyes land on? What most captures
your attention? Most likely, you'll find your gaze
directed to one point in particular, more than the others, and
it's something the photographer intended for you to notice. In
each photograph, this element, no matter what it is, has the same
name: the leading subject.

The leading subject is what makes a photograph memorable
to the viewer and what gives a photograph meaning. Simply
put, the subject is the true essence of the photo. The subject
creates context and intrigue. It's what propels the viewer to ask

questions or make assumptions about what is taking place in the photo or what its intended meaning is. The entirety of the photograph revolves around the subject, and without it, the story is untold.

The subject *is* the story, whether it's a person, place, or thing. Every photo has a unique story, and the narrative always stems from the subject. The story crafted by a photograph can be a complete description of its time, place, emotions, and history. Everything can be conveyed through the type of subject chosen and the way the subject is utilized in the photo.

I don't go anywhere without a camera. In my opinion, it doesn't matter what kind of camera you have as long as you bring it along. The best camera you have is always the one you have with you.[1] You never know when a subject will suddenly show itself.

A MAGICAL MOMENT

It was an early spring Saturday morning. My son had waited for this moment his entire life, he claimed, though he was four at the time. It was the home opener of his first season of baseball. (I can't call it T-ball because, after all, this was Texas.) So there we were, waiting for the parade of players. Parents flanked both sides of the field as they announced my son's team. "The Loooooooonghorns," said the gravelly voice, drawing out their name in a loud southern drawl over the PA system. It was like someone had shot a howitzer as the kids took off running past the crowd of cheering parents. There I was, slightly kneeling down. My finger poised on the shutter release, and then I saw it:

my son. My beautiful, ever-caring, comedic character of a son was leading the pack. *Click!*

If I were to look at the photo with a critical eye, it's not technically perfect by my standards; but despite that, there is something about it that makes it flawless to me. The excitement and energy bursting from my son's face could power a small Texas town for an entire year. I had never seen my son this happy. It was like Christmas, the Fourth of July, and his birthday all wrapped up into one.

There is something magical about my son in this picture, and it's more than simply the fact that he's my son. Even to a casual observer who doesn't have the obvious parental bias I do, the photo contains something special. My son's face is so full of joy that you can't look away, and you find yourself smiling right along with him. The thrill, the wonderment, the elation, the innocence, the pent-up excitement . . . you can feel it, and it reminds you of some of the thrills of your own childhood. I've spent a lot of time analyzing the photo, and I've realized that it's not the background or the shutter speed or the angle or the focus that makes this photo magical. There is one simple factor that makes it so striking: the sheer enjoyment of the leading subject, my son.

This photo without my son would be utterly pointless. Photoshop him out and what are you left with? A picture devoid of meaning, of feeling, of purpose. A photo without a subject is like a book without words . . . a song without a chorus . . . a ballpark frank without the hot dog. Without it there is no way to understand or decipher what the photographer is trying to say. No way to comprehend their point of view or what story they are trying to tell.

GLIMPSES INTO HISTORY

Beyond telling a story, photography is a glimpse of life itself. A split second of eternity, captured forever. It is a slice of someone's life that is suspended in time exactly as it was in that precise moment.

It is the job of the photographer to capture and produce this image of a single second of someone's life. The representation must be honest and true in regards to the subject and can, in some cases, be considered bold and direct. What the lens of a camera captures has a way of transcending time and space. I love the way Aaron Siskind puts it: "Photography is a way of feeling, of touching, of loving. What you have caught on film is captured forever . . . it remembers little things, long after you have forgotten everything."[2]

A brief, solitary flash captures a moment in time and encapsulates it, preserving the emotions, the occurrence, for years to come. Photographs both captivate and inform, showcasing a piece of humanity at a specific point in time and giving us glimpses into their lives and into the events of their era.

Do you remember Joe Rosenthal's iconic photograph of five United States marines and a US Navy corpsman raising the American flag during the Battle of Iwo Jima during World War II? That image depicts a single, victorious moment drawn from an incredibly difficult time in our nation's history. With little other distraction in the photo's background, it's easy to see what Rosenthal intended his subject to be: the soldiers. When we see them, struggling together to hoist the American flag and plant it firmly in the Japanese soil of Iwo Jima, we remember what the members of our armed forces were fighting for. By clearly identifying the photo's subjects and capturing them in a powerful setting, Rosenthal immortalized that moment in our country's history, and the image still speaks to us today.

LET YOUR SUBJECT SPEAK

And that's just it. Photographs speak to us. Sometimes they whisper nostalgic phrases, reminding us of days gone by and saturating our souls with warm memories, like a picture of your favorite toy from childhood. Sometimes they yell, "Pay attention to me! How will you respond to the horrors of what I am showing you?" as they lay out images of families in desperate circumstances from halfway around the world—or perhaps even more shockingly—from our own cities and neighborhoods. Sometimes images shout, "Hooray! This is how life was meant to be lived!" as they fill our hearts with pride at the sight of an elated child riding his bike for the first time or an Olympian crossing the finish line in first place.

There is so much a photograph can explain that, in many instances, is more effective than a written document. Do you find it any wonder that the most popular posts on Facebook are the ones that contain images?[3] Photos grab hold of our attention in ways that words sometimes cannot. Even lovers of the written word have acknowledged the power of images, igniting a rise in the popularity of typography.

Photographs speak. Their subjects call to us and beg us to look, to really look, at the messages buried within them. And the language of photographs is understood by all. The messages interpreted by the viewers may be varied, even opposing, yet they are there. We all see the subject from our own unique point of view, through our own lenses of understanding, from our own cultural perspectives, filtered through our own experiences and backgrounds. Yet the subject speaks. And it continues to speak to all who will listen.

SUBJECTS HELP US MAKES SENSE OF OUR WORLD

Photographs don't just help us understand moments from the past; they also help us to interpret moments and events that are happening today. These moments happen all the time, but we may not see them until that one image grabs our attention. In an instant, it pulls us back into reality. It grounds us and makes us ask, why?

I vividly remember on September 11 and the days following, seeing images of the World Trade Center crashing down in New York City and the faces of those who were at the site. When I looked into the eyes of a photograph's subject as she stared up in horror at the burning towers, her mouth partially covered by her hand, her hair and face covered in ash, I felt the impact of the devastation in a fresh way. Her eyes, her face, her posture, and her appearance all interpreted the event from a distinct angle and asked me to see what had happened from her perspective. We might hear stories of the millions of children dying of AIDS in Africa, but when we see a photograph that has chosen a Kenyan mother as its subject, a mother looking up to the heavens, tears streaming down her weathered face as she cradles her dead child in her arms in grief, we imagine what she must be feeling. In an instant, the story travels all the way from

Kenya into our living room and into our hearts, suddenly not so far away.

Photographs not only help us interpret our world, but they also, for years to come, remind us of what we have lived through. Nowadays, when I see a powerful image of the burning Twin Towers, it brings me back in time in a split second. I can close my eyes and see exactly where I was standing at the moment I saw the breaking story on TV. When those who are old enough to remember the assassination of JFK see a picture of him in his car on that fateful day, they can instantly describe to you where they were when they heard the news. While the spoken and written word announces and informs, a single photograph of those events serves as a staunch reminder of those terrible days. I believe the most evocative stories are told through pictures and are the lasting symbols of times gone by.

WHEN THE SUBJECT IS PERSONAL

Photographs can also bring us healing and offer escape. In times of grief, it is important to have a lasting memento of someone lost. A photograph can hearken back to times of happiness and other fond memories. It offers a respite of the emotional turmoil set in motion by your loss.

My grandparents were incredibly special people in my life. But time is cruel in that it tends to blur and cloud memories and images of faces that were once crystal-clear in our minds. Photographs recalibrate those images and stories, making them fresh and clear once again. When I see the photo of me tending to the American flag outside their home as my grandfather watched on because he was too frail to retire Old Glory, or his military photographs from Burma that show him goofing off with his army Air Corps buddies, I remember how great a man he was. I can picture him sitting there in his overstuffed reclining chair as I sat across from him on the couch as he told me tale after tale of his own childhood—his wild fraternity stories at Penn State, or the time he began playing tennis because of a certain girl when he transferred to Oklahoma Teachers College (now Oklahoma State University).

When I look at my favorite picture of the two of them posing for our church directory—he in his staple uniform of a black suit with a burgundy tie, and his barrel-shaped, wide-rimmed glasses . . . her with her perfectly done hair and loving disposition . . . my grandmother slightly looking up out of the corner of her eye at her husband's face with a half-smile . . . he looking back at her with a flirtatious grin—I remember the love they had for each other. I remember the hardships my granddad endured fighting in World War II, the way he would tease us all mercilessly and make us laugh, and the smile he would share with my grandmother, as though they were in their own little world—a place of eternal love and adoration. The small gestures he would do for her, just to see her smile, were the things I remember most clearly. And it all rushes back to my mind as though they had never left, all because of a single photograph. They were the subjects, and I, the grateful receiver. Ansel Adams says, "A great photograph is a full expression of what one feels about what is being photographed in the deepest sense, and is, thereby, a true expression of what one feels about life in its entirety."[4]

It is the photographs themselves that give meaning to our lives. They portray our lives, whether good or bad. They capture our relationships as they change and grow and adapt and end . . . all the places we have gone and the memories of what we did there and how we felt at the time . . . each event we celebrated and each moment of glory all captured and kept for all time.

There are typically pictures taken of the most important events in a person's life—a whole series of photos in which *you* are the subject. When you were born, your mom or dad snapped away. The camera was pulled out when you had a birthday, graduated from school, got married, or celebrated any significant events or accomplishments. And if your parents weren't very handy with a camera, you may have grown up with a determination that you would capture these moments in your own life or in the lives of your children.

Then we put these photographs, our collection of precious moments, into albums and hard drives, boxes, and frames. We surround ourselves with our memories and want them readily accessible. We choose the photos that tell the stories of our lives best and frame them, letting the subjects speak to anyone who walks in the room and sees them.

We keep these photographs as a testament of our lives and leave them behind as legacies for future generations. They are the story of our lives, all wrapped up in photo albums or electronic folders. They are our way of telling and showing others who we are and what we have done. They are one way we share our story.

SUBJECTS SHARE STORIES

This ability to share our stories is why I love and appreciate photography. An image, correctly captured, can be the voice for the voiceless and hope to the hopeless. By conveying the reality of the human condition, photography can create light in the darkness.

Because photographs don't require a common vocabulary, they speak a universal language. Your views, stories, and thoughts can be shared with someone halfway across the world without having to know one syllable of each other's vernacular. As Orson Welles says, "The camera is much more than a recording apparatus; it is a medium via which messages reach us from another world."[5]

Your subjects speak without using a single word.

Though it may seem cliché, photographs really are worth a thousand words—and maybe even much more. Each photograph is a complete story and sometimes cannot be explained in words alone. It's difficult to explain one photograph with a single word, but we can explain many words with one photograph. Edward Steichen says, "Photography records the gamut of feelings written on the human face, the beauty of the earth and skies that man has inherited, and the wealth and confusion man has created. It is a major force in explaining man to man."[6]

Photographs are timeless, wordless, soundless pieces of our lives.

In times of disaster, people generally attempt to save their photographs first. When we lose our photographs, we feel that we've lost a part of ourselves—a part of our stories. Because we and our families are the primary subjects in our photographs, when we lose our photos, it's as if we are watching moments of our lives wisp up with the smoke of fire. Whether it's fire, floods, hurricanes, or tornadoes, people are willing to take huge risks to save their most cherished possessions, and their most prized possessions usually include photographs.

Homes, clothes, other material things—they're all replaceable. But photographs are irreplaceable; they are one of a kind. People are willing to dive back into a burning house or risk getting caught in the storm in order to save the photos that record their legacy and history. We believe it's worth the threat of danger. Have you ever looked at a photograph and said, "I completely forgot about that! I haven't thought about that in years!"? We are terrified of losing photos because we know if they disappear, the memories they are associated with may just disappear too. Our photos capture moments that are gone forever, impossible to reproduce. We are creatures made of memories, defined by experiences, built upon by each moment of our lives.

I distinctly remember covering the aftermath of a tornado in Minnesota some years back. The image of an uprooted tree sitting in the middle of a living room of a small house while destruction ran havoc all around it is burned into my memory.

The large pieces of vinyl siding from the house were strewn across the small farming town like discarded Popsicle sticks. I was taking in all of the destruction when I saw a woman scouring the fallen debris, frantically searching for the photographs she had tucked away in her closets and shelves.

The devastation was all around her, but the thing she was most afraid of was the loss of her memories and legacy in the form of photographs. I remember her saying in an interview, "I could replace everything but my photos; they tell my life's story." Those precious memories she had spent her life gathering and storing were the one thing she couldn't recreate, because once the moment has passed, it can never be accessed again.

YOU ARE GOD'S SUBJECT

Photographs are a lasting reminder of what has come to pass, whether good or bad. They can bring comfort in tough times and joy in simple times. They are, in a sense, a vivid story imprinted on the humble material of paper and plastic. If you think about it, we are no different.

Our Creator is the photographer and we are his subjects—brilliant projections that our God and Creator has built to stand in a certain context. We are his foci placed in the contexts of suffering and hardship, and he means for us to shine and project beauty and light.

Just as we are photographers, capturing images through the lens of a camera, cementing that image for all time, so, too, are we depictions to others of life and love for God. After he released his shutter in the sky, creating us and placing his divine signature on our lives, we became his representations, made in his image as living expressions of his holy presence in humanity. He is always there as a part of the human narrative and stands right beside us and shines through us as we stand tall in the theater of suffering.

God works through you and me, just as he has worked through so many others mentioned in the Bible. I recall a time when God worked through me to withstand this world of woe. I was walking home from class one cold day during my freshman year of college. There on the side of the sidewalk, tucked in the entryway of a storefront to shelter himself from the elements, was a man who clearly had no home. Seeing his deeply matted hair and smelling a disturbing odor emitting from his body, I involuntarily pulled away from him.

To be honest, I was repulsed by his appearance. He was ragged and dirty—surely he had some sort of disease—so I had decided to swing wide of him on the sidewalk. But then something happened. Something quickened inside me as if a divine presence was filling me and I was compelled to do the work of God. I knelt down next to this man—this creation of God—and dropped twenty dollars into his small, worn paper cup.

When he looked up at me, I could see the pure gratitude he had for me, a stranger who had helped him when no one else would. The feeling that filled me at that moment was indescribable; the only thing I can say was that I knew that God was there, working through me and with me. It was a moment that filled my soul. I didn't have a camera with me that day, and even if I had, it would have been inappropriate to take a picture of him. But with my eyes as my lens, I centered my subject's face in my mental viewfinder and snapped an image of what I saw that day, and thankfully it is an image I can still recall.

That day he was the subject of my mental photograph. *Every* day, he is the subject of God's.

This ability of people to feel the divine grace of God flowing through them and working in conjunction with them is a blessing bestowed onto humanity by God's glory. But I am not alone in this venture—many throughout the Bible have been equally blessed by God's grace.

Photographs are just one of many mediums that can be used to tell a story. God chose to pass on this one greatest story of all (told in the form of many smaller stories) to us in the form of narrative, which was then recorded in the written word. And just as photographs have a subject, so do narratives, and God's stories are no exception. When you open the Bible, you can see how God developed central characters in the New Testament to expand his kingdom and spread his gospel. But one of the most beautiful things about God's story is that it is still being lived out. We are the modern-day disciples he has chosen as the subjects of the stories he is writing through our lives.

I love how artist Francis Bacon imagines Jesus: "Jesus would have been one of the best photographers that ever existed. He was always looking at the beauty of people's souls. In fact, Jesus was constantly making pictures of God in people's life by looking at their souls and exposing them to his light."[7]

This quote reminds me of the story in Acts when Saul literally saw the light on his way to Damascus.[8] Saul was a man who was repulsed by Jesus and his followers. As a matter of fact, he was carrying letters from the high priest to synagogues in Damascus giving him the authority to arrest any followers of Jesus he found.[9] Saul was so intent on opposing the name of Jesus of Nazareth that in raging fury, he threatened to murder the disciples.[10]

So here was a guy who had disdain dripping from his pores for Christ and all who were associated with him, when he was blinded by a bright light and heard a voice saying, "I am Jesus from Nazareth whom you are persecuting . . . get up and go to Damascus. There you will be told about all the things I have planned for you to do."[11] Blind as a bat, Saul had to be led by his companions into Damascus. For several days, all he could do was pray. Finally, God sent Ananias to visit Saul, where he put his hands on Saul and prayed for him. Instantly, Saul could see again and became a man who began to tell his story and his love for Jesus and, ultimately, changed his name to Paul.[12]

God exposed Saul to his light because he knew that Saul

would change his mind once Christ changed his heart. He could not deny being blinded by the light of God nor his incomprehensible healing. What I love most about this story is that when you read the thirteen books that Paul wrote in the Bible, you begin to see how he was one of God's main subjects. It's as if each book he penned points back to that time on the road to remind us of God's will and what Ananias spoke to him: "You will be his witness to all people, telling them about what you have seen and heard."[13]

Remember the pictographs of the Plains Indians that I referred to earlier in the book? The pictographs were a living witness of the tribe's most significant events: harsh winters, famine, the supernatural, and the natural occurrences that happened each year. The keepers knew the vital importance of passing on the stories of their tribes from one generation to another. We also find visual markers like this in the Bible—such as when God said the Israelites should tie several pieces of thread together and intertwine a single blue thread to form a tassel, then attach it to the hem of their clothing so every time they would see the tassel they would be reminded to follow God and not their desires, which they were prone to do.[14] God knows we often need a visual reminder.

All these stories are like letters bearing witness to generations that came after them—their subjects help to frame our existence and provide us with a point of reference. These messages from the past call our attention; they add perspective and focus the narrative of a community.

These works develop a composition that allows for deeper processing of past events and that can also be used as a guide for potential future events. Events that have happened in one's past stand as pillars of a transformational story just waiting to be told.

Equally, the stories of our past stand as images of our own history. Just as a photographer tells a story with an image, may our own lives produce direct and honest representations of our lives that inspire others to live in a way that brings glory to God.

CREATED IN GOD'S IMAGE

How humbling it is to be chosen by God as his subjects. Sometimes it's hard to believe that he wants *us* to be his representation—that he thinks *we* are capable of showing others who he is. Let the great honor of these words ring in your heart and never lose their wonder: *you are created in the image of God.*[15] He looks at you with the same awe and tenderness that I look at my son within that classic photo of him at his first T-ball game. He looks at you and he smiles. He gazes with delight at what he has made and thinks, *Indeed, it is very good.*[16]

The more we become aware of God's great love and his incredible plans for us and through us, the more we are transformed from the inside out to reflect and possess his image. Every day our conversations, our actions, our responses, and our love or lack of it, are creating snapshots in the minds of others. When they think of us, what image will come to mind? What mental photo of us will they see? Let's not only take great photos, but let's *make* great photos with our lives. God sees the big picture and is carefully working behind the scenes, crafting our lives and weaving them into his divine composition.

NINE

COMPOSITION

Composition is the strongest way of seeing.

—EDWARD WESTON

Has this ever happened to you? You're somewhere with your camera in hand, ready to take a photo. Maybe you're walking through a beautiful old town with historic buildings, or you're at an event filled with opportunities for action-packed shots. Suddenly you see it—the perfect composition. An image forms in your mind and you lift your camera, eager to recreate the scene you just imagined. Excitedly you snap away, knowing you got it. But later, when you view the images you captured, your eyebrows furrow with frustration. These pictures look nothing like what you thought they would! What happened?

It's happened to all of us—whether you're a photographer

who bombed a photo shoot, a musician who had the perfect song in her head in the car but found it sounding quite less-than-perfect when she played it on her guitar, or a writer thinking out loud whose phrases sounded significantly less profound once he wrote them down. Or maybe it's as simple as composing a killer tweet in the shower only to later realize how dumb it actually sounds typed out in 140 characters.

We all seek to compose in one way or another—to take many elements and carefully capture or craft them into one piece of brilliant beauty. Sometimes it works, and sometimes it doesn't.

For every good photograph that photographers take, they have a much greater pile of images that were slightly out of focus, the exposure was set too high or too low, they had the wrong angle, or probably more than most would like to admit, the composition was just off.

Composition is one of the most vital ingredients that goes into a great photograph or into any creative outlet. It's the divine code that frames the scene, brings the story to life, draws attention to the subject, and adds balance and harmony. *Composition, at its core, is the act of putting together or combining parts or ingredients into artistic form.*

However, the true magic of composition is all in the framing, it's the subtle nuance of knowing the image is just right; it's something that has to be learned from practicing, rather than following hard-and-fast rules in some textbook. And even if you follow all the "rules" of composition, sometimes a photograph can just end up utterly stale.

Finding the secret sauce is a bit of trial and error. I call it the dance of discontent. It's why when you see photographers working, they look like they have ants in their pants. They're bouncing around from place to place. Squatting. Kneeling. Lying on things. Standing on their tiptoes. In order to find the perfect balance and composition they must constantly move, forever on a quest for the best frame—exploring their surroundings for just the right angle. It's the subtle position of a ballerina . . . the look on her face . . . the way her arms are raised just so. And every millisecond, each of those details changes as the camera rapidly and repetitively captures the subject frame by frame—each image so similar yet so very different. The slightest shift in her stance or facial expression can bring the image and moment to life—having a striking impact on the final prodcut. The dance yields a collection of similar depth of fields, multiple scenes, and angles to find the perfect composition.

Composition doesn't seem like it would be that hard. But the reality is, as with most things in life, it's far more difficult than it sounds. The devil is in the details—something I didn't know when I started out in photography.

MY FIRST CAMERA, COMPOSERS, AND SHOTGUN SHELLS

I remember getting my first camera in second grade. It was a Kodak Colorburst 100 Instant Camera—the Kodak version of a Polaroid. I remember my parents immediately telling me, "Don't take too many pictures," because the film for that thing was expensive! They gave me that advice because there was a real cost involved every time I took a photo. Little did they know there was great wisdom for life to be found in their simple words.

I remember blowing through the first pack of film ten minutes after opening the camera—so much for listening.

I quickly realized the many varying factors that went into each image I captured. Everything needed to be important. The light . . . because if it was too dark you couldn't make out the scene. The balance of the subjects . . . so my dad didn't look like a tree was growing out of his head. The framing . . . so I didn't end up chopping off the arm of the person on the left of the group shot. And the final lesson my parents imparted to me was to "hold the camera still," after they looked at shot after shot of blurry pictures I had taken. These early lessons helped shape both the importance of composition and meaning behind the photos I took and the world around me.

Since then, I've gone to great lengths and complexity to see the natural composition as if through the eyes of a child. I dig deep to unearth the weight and balance of my image so that I can bring a level of interest, dominance, and influence into my frame. Like a composer arranging music for an orchestra, I bring harmony into the scene by adding depth to produce an aesthetically complex image. Like life, there is also the evocative play between unity and diversity. And hopefully, if I executed all of that correctly, I have a composition that tells a story.

While I shoot digital images now, I still ration my shutter to take only images that stand against the test of time. For some, taking photos is like holding down the trigger on a machine gun—you hold down the shutter and capture twelve images in a second, leaving captured images strewn across your memory card like spent shotgun shells on the ground. For me, taking a photograph has holy significance. It is a likeness, and in that, it stands for something much, much more. The pictures I create are not the same ones I photographed—they are more; they are images that matter and stretch one's feelings and experiences. Each image says something about my identity and who I am.

A photographer is like a musician arranging notes in a grand opus to bring emotion and a sense of meaning from his compositional framing. He is, in many ways, choosing the way we see the story by determining what is placed in the frame and what is left out. A photographer also chooses what is aesthetically pleasing and what has meaning based on the mood and emotion in the moment.

WHEN WE ARE OUR OWN COMPOSERS

Sometimes I feel like our lives are a lot like Pinterest. We collect things without really linking the importance of the quaint, beautiful, and touching things we find. We pin for involvement. We pin to connect. We pin to express ourselves. We pin to share our philosophies with others. We pin to dream. We pin to create. We pin to bring our lives meaning.

Pin a photo of Hanscom's Bakery in New York City taken in 1939 by János Albók. Pin an antique dresser given a fresh shot at life via some sandpaper and a new paint job. Pin the quote, "It is well with my soul," overlaid onto a photo of an anchor. And don't forget the obligatory pin of a "someecard" for good measure.

The snapshot of our current culture is of a people desperately trying to be unique, to make a place in this world, to have an identity. People can get to know us by seeing what we project about ourselves on the collage boards that are our LinkedIn profiles, our Facebook timelines, our Twitter pages, our Behance profiles, our Pinterest pages, or our Instagram feeds. Each site portrays a slightly different view of us, customized for the audience who will see it. We are composers of ourselves.

Reality is hidden behind the carefully constructed. There is true beauty to be found, but the artificial coating obstructs our views of one another like Vaseline smeared on our glasses. Sometimes our self-projections are very intentional, like those found on our online résumés. But many other times, we pin or tweet out faster than we can think, focusing on how we feel in the moment rather than how these projections of ourselves will affect others' perceptions of us—in many cases sending out an anthem that comes across as ambiguous.

The result of these many self-projections can end up relegating our view of composition to interest instead of the whole picture, if we let it. Rather than taking the time to get to know the real us—the unique creatures God made us to be—the temptation is to fill our time with real-time tweeting, liking, pinning, posting, and Instagramming and then measuring all the feedback to shape who we *should* become.

Ask yourself these questions:

- "What have I told the world about who I am?"
- "Is it true?"
- "Why do I want them to see me this way?"
- "Are my self-compositions more intentional or spontaneous?"

AN IDENTITY CRISIS

Our world is made up of patterns, textures, and lines. A photographer is able to see how the parts can make a beautiful whole—an image. Likewise, we are composed of various parts that God combines and builds in his image. He is our photographer, and we are his compositions. He breathed life into dirt, spoke into the air, formed our souls, and then offered his perfect love to whoever would have him. He imagined us. He created us. He loved us. He transformed us. He filled us.

We often struggle to see the true composition and framing around us, because most of us want to be unique. We are not sure we want to see things for what they really are. We struggle in the tension between wanting to be who God created us to be and feeling frustrated with the way he made us. We would rather be like the guy who has the sport coat with patches on the elbows, who drives a 1940 Alfa Romeo and has style oozing from his pores. Like Pinterest, we pin a little gospel here, a little Ryan Gosling there, a little bow tie here, and a Scripture verse there. We do this because we're uncomfortable in our own skin. We do this to dream and to be accepted, and deep down we have the hope of being different.

The truth about ourselves is not always pleasing, and most times we try to avoid it at all costs. We distort the truth—sometimes a little, sometimes a lot—it often seems like a better and more unconventional path to take than putting the truth above ourselves. Let's be honest: sometimes we want to appear better than we really are more than we want to be completely truthful with ourselves. William Shakespeare pensively penned, "God has given us one face, and we make ourselves another."[1]

We want to look good. We want to be accepted. It's part of our DNA—yet it doesn't bring us lasting joy. And in these moments we choose to settle for inflating our egos, altogether missing the meaning of our lives. We were all born unique, but most of us will die copies.[2]

Paul writes three verses in Romans 8 that speak volumes to our identity. "The true children of God are those who let God's Spirit lead them. The Spirit we received does not make us slaves again to fear; it makes us children of God. With that Spirit we cry out, 'Father.' And the Spirit himself joins with our spirits to say we are God's children."[3]

This passage illustrates the internal battle with fear and insecurity that plagues us. It shows us God is affirming our identity in him. We oftentimes struggle with fear and a need to validate and establish ourselves because we don't feel we are connecting with God, but God will establish us and affirm our identity in him if we embrace the relationship. Outside of God, there is an identity vacuum that wreaks havoc in our lives if we let it, creating anxiety, depression, and insecurity within us. But when we let ourselves be wrapped up inside our Father's love, he reminds us that there is only one identity that matters: we are his children.

NEW EYES

When we begin our spiritual journey, we should examine ourselves under a microscope to see what we're made of; I think we'd be surprised at what we would find. God has made us for himself; our hearts are restless until they rest in him.[4] We need to view our lives through new eyes—through the eyes of our Creator—otherwise we'll be blind. We are his masterpieces and his magnum opus. In a real sense, rather than being formed *in* God's image, because God has no human image, we are created *as* God's image, or rather to be God's image and representative of the invisible.[5] Each of us represents God in a unique and different way. None of us on our own can wholly represent the fullness of God, so he has placed pieces of himself in each one of us and filled us with his Spirit. We are God's handiwork—we've been created to do good works, which God prepared in advance for us to do.[6]

We find this distinction by finding our "place" in Christ—not by differences in our physicality or appearance or geographical locations. Outside of Christ, we look to be defined by our worldly passing and temporal features, but all of these are empty. Our distinction is found in our place of service in Christ. He defines us as his children, and we engage others with our gifts. This is finding one's place in the family of God and giving up vain and empty forms of identification.[7]

There is something about our identification with Christ that elevates us. Fear sinks us. The story of Peter engaging with Christ, sharing in his glory and expressing his power by walking on the water with him is so powerful. It paints a picture for us of God's desire that we also share in Christ's power and elevated place of expressing God through our lives. When we divert our focus, we sink. We get into trying to prove ourselves and trying to work harder, and we are merely treading water like everyone else on the planet. But when we stop and look at him, behold him, identify with him, and trust him, we discover who we really are in him and are able to see ourselves as the Father sees us.

Trying to glimpse the fullness of the lives God has composed for us feels like straining our eyes to see a painting hanging on a wall on the other side of a huge auditorium and then being asked to describe what we see. And it's so much more than just standing in front of a mirror looking at ourselves. Have you ever looked at your children and marveled at how amazing they were, knowing they have so much inside them that they don't even realize yet? How much more does God see in us, as our Father? He created every fiber of our beings and knows every day—every moment—of our lives from beginning to end. Can we trust him? Can we let his feelings about us be more important to us than how others view us? Instead of tightly gripping the paintbrush of our lives, can we slowly relax our fingers, let go, and place it in his hands? Can we have faith in his goodness, his wisdom, and his love for us?

Living by faith and giving up one's own will are the first steps on the voyage of true identity. As we embark on our journeys, may our spiritual sails be filled with the strong wind of God's presence as we sail into unknown waters. As Marcel Proust says, "The real voyage of discovery consists not in seeing new landscapes, but in having new eyes."[8] God encourages us to step out of the boat and be what he designed us to be. We are a unique creation, and our gifts are designed to benefit the world in a real and meaningful way.

PART OF A GRAND COMPOSITION

Yes, we are each unique compositions made by God himself, but lest we become too self-focused, we must remember that we are all also pieces of a greater composition—the composition that makes up the beautiful, saving plan God has for all humankind. Just as any parent with more than one child knows, mothers and fathers deeply love each of their children as individuals, and all of their children, as the whole that makes up their family.

If you have ever taken a portrait of a family or participated in a family portrait session with a photographer, you know that often families want a variety of different shots and poses in different combinations. They want a group shot of everyone, a shot of each individual child, a shot of the daughters and mothers, then fathers and sons, the grandparents with their grandchildren, the siblings, the parents . . . and the list goes on.

Why do families do this? Because people were meant to exist in relationships. The solo shots represent the unique composition and splendor of the individual. The shot of the child with her parents tells us of the love that they have for her, as her "creators," protectors, and nurturers. The image of the entire family together shows the beauty of the whole—how each of the many members together makes up a grand composition that is one family.

And God is the Father of us all, of his one family, consisting of many members—each one of us. He cares about both our relationship with him directly and about our relationships with fellow Christians. As does any parent, he longs for unity, for love, and for a sense of team and togetherness.

Whether we are aware of it or not, we have each been created with talents and gifts unique to us that were meant not to be kept to ourselves but to be shared with the larger body of Christ. What kind of beauty can you bring to this world as an integral part of it? What can you share with those around you to help enrich their lives and bring them closer to their Father? In God's grand composition of this world, are you willing to let him use you to make it more beautiful?

The choices that we make have a direct impact on the quality of our expression of God. If we ignore God or his call, we will live in conflict with ourselves and never truly be satisfied. Without God in our lives we can't live up to the possibilities that he has in store for us. Despite all our accomplishments, without him, we will never be the people that deep inside we know we could be.

It is only when we can discover our value and identity in Christ that we are able to find our purpose and his pleasure. We need to see ourselves through God's lens. Instead of focusing on how we personally see ourselves, we need to concentrate on seeing ourselves through the same lens that God sees us— as the cherished children he created us to be.[9] Give the world what it's missing . . . you! Otherwise you and I lose ourselves by not finding places of service and by resisting our call to bring more meaning and hope to others' lives. By rejecting our part, we lose ourselves.

That meaning springs from finding ourselves present in the stories of others. Sometimes we think that being a part of someone else's story reduces our value—that being in the limelight is how value is gathered. The truth is that when we descend into depths of service and engagement with a heart for others, we find our gifts and energy truly come to life, making our purpose more apparent.

Like developing a photo, when we choose to trust God with our lives, our uniqueness comes into vivid focus. Our lives are like film; there is a cost—an eternal cost—and we shouldn't ruin them by doing things we don't really want to be doing. By focusing on the things that matter, we are at liberty to be our best selves. We were created by God to be different—each of us a unique expression. By choosing to trust God with our lives, we express those unique individualities more fully with our lives, enhancing not only our lives but the lives of those around us. Let's be active participators in God's work of creation, letting him continually mold us into who he made us to be and partnering with him in bringing his love to others, creating a composition more complex and beautiful than we ever could have imagined.

PART THREE

DEVELOP

TEN

PROCESSING

Life is a lively process of becoming.

—Gen. Douglas MacArthur

If you haven't figured out by now, I'm unique. I see things differently. I look at things through an extraordinary filter, and it's a skill that I'm deeply grateful for because it has come in handy in my profession. Whether I'm telling the story of a missionary or rebranding and defining a company's ethos, I've been blessed with the ability to understand situations and people, along with a distinctive way of processing experiences.

The way I look at things has become almost ritualistic in my life—like how after a photo or video shoot I orchestrate a unique, delicate dance of data and pixels, where I look back through my media and meditate on the moments I captured to find the best images or sequences that give shape to the story I'm telling.

I look closely for any unintentional fuzziness. Yes, I admit I may be excessively compulsive, but if parts of the picture are sharp while other parts are out of focus and it's not clear that it was not supposed to be that way, I feel it can ruin a picture and its story. I spend a lot of time examining each scene for clutter. I want to make sure nothing will spoil the composition by distracting focus away from the main subject. I spend time following lines, making sure there aren't several points of interest that battle with one another for a viewer's attention. I look at the highlighting, the exposure, and the coloring to make sure the image is properly lit. I press on, making sure there are no unflattering facial expressions.

For me, each photo I take needs to say something very clearly. The message and the meaning cannot be ambiguous. The images shape my half-articulated feelings, casting light into my inner depths and exposing my deepest, truest self.

The way I process my work is a reflection of how I process life.

DECIDING WHAT TO DO WITH MY DISABILITY

In second grade, I was diagnosed with an "auditory processing disorder"—a type of learning disability. In its purest form, my brain processes information drastically differently than most. Growing up I had difficulty with reading and comprehension. Additionally, I had trouble paying attention and remembering information that was presented orally. I remember feeling a large amount of frustration because I knew something was wrong and that it was hard for me to focus. I think what made it more prevalent was that my classmates knew something was out of the ordinary as well because I read differently than most. Nicely put, you could say I took my time reading.

I. Read. Each. Word. Slowly. To. Make. Sure. I. Pronounced. It. Correctly.

I'm sure I sounded like a cross between Ben Stein in *Ferris Bueller's Day Off*—"Bueller . . ."—and a monotone robot, but I did this because I needed more time to process information than other kids in my class. And so, as kids are so prone to do at that age, my classmates made fun of me every time I was called to read out loud. It was a confusing time for me because there was so much to process. I learned quickly who my friends were. I was coping with feeling broken or faulty because I had trouble learning the "right way," or the way the system dictated.

What I learned on my own through this time was that true learning was reflected in the way I responded to environmental, social, emotional, and physical stimuli—by the way I came to understand new things. Robert Bennett says, "Your life is the sum result of all the choices you make, both consciously and unconsciously. If you can control the process of choosing, you can take control of all aspects of your life. You can find the freedom that comes from being in charge of yourself."[1] I chose to let my learning style be defined by my ease in processing visual information—rather than my difficulty with processing auditory things. In other words, I focused on my strengths, not my weaknesses. And in that choosing, I found freedom.

I am an intensely visual learner, and I began to learn to embrace that. I had tried to learn by listening, but each time I felt overwhelmed by distractions and unable to focus. So instead, I let myself learn by watching and reflecting back on situations and dissecting them to figure out meaning and context. When trying to remember something, I would call up images from the past. My head was constantly swimming with three-dimensional pictures and images that I used to make sense of life. I learned to look at problems and visualize multiple situations and scenarios that would point me in the right direction.

As I took notes in class, I illustrated them. When I wanted to understand a concept better, I drew pictures to help me visualize the information. I spent a large portion of my time mentally processing all I had taken down before and after my classes, reviewing and organizing my notes. It was at this time in my life that I discovered my love for simplicity and minimalism, which helped me focus and stay consistent to prevent overload. All of this tied together to help me sort out information in a way that was meaningful and personal, helping me concentrate and not get distracted.

The more I dove into my visual strengths, the more I realized that the way I saw and processed things differently was actually a strength rather than a weakness. I was able to see past the two-dimensional scene playing out in front of me and pinpoint a new perspective. I paid attention to body language, facial expressions, and the subtle details that often get buried, and I learned to perceive what someone was feeling or experiencing without even asking him or her.

At the time, what I didn't realize was that God was up to something. What I saw as a hurdle or a malfunctioning part of my being was actually a divine path God had carved out for me to be able to process things in a way that revealed hidden and deeper meanings—to be able to find the rest of the story not always visible to the casual onlooker.

CONNECTING WITH GOD IN UNCONVENTIONAL WAYS

I'll never forget this one time in my early thirties when I was starving for direction. In my mind, I felt like I was completely lost—just going through the motions and hoping something would come up. I had been feeling spiritually dry and had been struggling to connect with God. I remember one morning, sitting on the edge of the chair in my office, staring at the images I was posting on my computer screen—willing myself to concentrate as I tried to force inspiration and keep pressing forward, when I finally gave up. I heaved a deep, soul-wrenching sigh and dropped my forehead into my hands as one of those half-thought/half-prayers whispered through my spirit: *God, I miss you. I know you're here with me, but for some reason I feel far away from you. I don't like feeling this way. Where are you? I want to be with you. Will you help me?*

I didn't think much more about it after that—in fact, I forgot all about my whispered prayer until I found myself standing in front of "The Colonel," a very wise spiritual guy who seems tapped into God more than anyone I know. I've come to realize there are plenty of ways God speaks to us, and hearing from God isn't a matter of whether he's speaking, but whether we are listening. So, in that moment, God began to move—not in a disruptive expansive way but more like when the wind sweeps down in a subtle, nudging way. A comforting way. It was as if The Colonel knew what I was dealing with and how I was as feeling. He placed his hand on my shoulder and said, "I know you feel you don't matter, that God dropped you into this new journey and now he's abandoned you. And you're trying to connect with him, but you feel like there is nothing but silence."

He continued, "Let me just reassure you that God is anything but silent. He is pervasive and ever present. Just because he may or may not have responded to a prayer or your call to him does not mean he didn't hear you or he doesn't care. He will respond. God is not silent, Matt. Sometimes the answers coming from God are much deeper than words because what he is saying is not on the surface level of life."

I stood there in amazement. God had heard my prayer and had met me right where I was, talking to me in the language my soul speaks. I went home and picked up my Bible and sat quietly with my Father for about twenty minutes, thanking him for being faithful to me, even when I hadn't been faithful to him. I felt his goodness wash over me and a fresh and renewed energy to connect with him. As he promises us in his Word, "When you search for me with all your heart, you will find me!"[2] I remembered that God wasn't far from me; he wasn't hard to find—he was simply a prayer away. Sometimes the only way God can get our attention and teach us something is to allow the events in our lives to guide us to and through the exact things we need to discover.

Time for a moment of authenticity: I have a hard time picking up my Bible. I have a hard time trying to focus on reading with all that is going on around me at a given time. It takes practice, just like the meticulous nuances of processing an image. Most artists work hard to express themselves with their gift. They paint and shade until the contrast is just right. They compose, fighting with the melody for the perfect, soul-catching sound. They write with detailed precision in an attempt to make sure every word counts, so that only the backspace key knows the true work that has been put into a sentence. This all takes years to perfect and thousands upon thousands of hours of dedicated focus. But the love these artists have for their craft and passion and how they feel about their work fuels them to push and struggle and pursue.

For some people, pursuing God comes as naturally to them as editing an image comes to me. Their relationship with God is the raw image on the table, and they continually examine and refine it and better it, using his Word as their editing tool. As they bathe themselves in his presence, as they study and wrestle with the true meaning of Scriptures, as they discuss their findings with others and attempt to live out what they are discovering, their lives become more and more beautiful and Christlike.

I've watched these people admittedly with a bit of envy, wishing that I had the same drive and desire that they did for God. Wishing that my hand craved the feel of his Word in its grip the same way it craves cradling a camera. Have you ever felt that way?

There have been so many times that I've picked up the Word or sat in a church service and all of the sudden, I am a second-grader all over again, struggling to process and then articulate what is in front of me. But God is not a narrow-minded teacher who has provided only three ways of getting to know him, and if you have difficulty reading, listening or sitting quietly, then *too bad for you!* God is aware of how we are made. He knows our ins and outs. He knows exactly how we learn and process information. And he has not hidden himself from us. Remember, his promise to us is, "When you search for me with all your heart, you will find me!"

Now, I could use my auditory processing disorder as an excuse to give up. *Why read God's Word? I can't focus. Why go to church? I can't pay attention. Why sit quietly before God? My mind won't stay still.* Or I could focus on my strength—the gift of visual perception that God has given me—and see how I can use that to seek the One I love.

I had a choice growing up: do I quit school because of my learning difficulties? Do I sit in college lectures and then get up and march out in frustration when the speaker drones on in a way that is not conducive to my way of learning? I chose to answer those questions with a resounding *no.* I figured out how to use my strengths to adapt. I illustrated my notes. I visualized what the professor was saying. I created doodles in the margins of my textbooks that pointed back to key points. Why did I go to such a great effort? Because I knew the end result was worth it. It *wasn't* easy, but it *was* worth it. I cared about what was being taught, and I knew that as I learned it, that information would help me become the creative I so badly wanted to be. I was propelled by my passion, fueled by the fire within, motivated by what I imagined lay ahead. Nothing was going to hold me back.

What legitimate excuse is holding you back from having a thriving relationship with God? How can you see the flip side of that weakness as a strength—a strength God can work through to show himself to you?

Have you had the privilege of seeing either *St. John's Bible* by Donald Jackson or *The Four Holy Gospels* by Makoto Fujimura? Both of these stunning renditions of Scripture, illustrated with original works of art, are examples of how individuals chose to express their relationship with God and to his Word by illuminating the text visually. These artists were as passionate, if not more, about knowing and understanding their Creator, as they were about the creative talents they had been blessed with. Or have you seen Ed's Story, a series of short films by Flannel.org? They tell the story of Ed's diagnosis with ALS, how he's been given a short time to live, and how suffering changes us for better or worse. These short films are beautifully shot, incredibly well written, excellently executed . . . but above all else, they are spiritual. And I'm sure you can think of examples of your own of people who sought God and expressed him in unique and wonderful ways that came out of their places of strength.

God will connect with us where we are in ways that we understand. He loves it when we process our faith in ways that reflect our personalities and strengths. After all, we are made in his image, so those strengths that we have? We get them from our Dad. He gets us, because he made us. No question is too crazy, no struggle too strong, no heart cry too loud for him.

STRUGGLING, SEEKING, AND SEEING

God not only permits but even wants us to enter into a realm that in some cases has a lot of question marks. A place where we struggle. A place where we strive to see things not outwardly visible. He wants us to look at things differently. To go deeper. To not merely read his Word at the surface level. He wants us to wonder. To observe. To see without presupposing. He wants us to process our observations, to meditate on them, and with them, frame our faith. Our most beautiful works, many times, come stained with the most blood, sweat, and tears. Out of the struggle are birthed new revelations, new perspectives, and new life.

Framing our faith produces roots in our lives. It grounds

us when we process our experiences and life through the Word. "His delight is in the law of the LORD, and in His law he meditates day and night. He shall be like a tree planted by the rivers of water, that brings forth its fruit in its season, whose leaf also shall not wither; and whatever he does shall prosper."[3]

Sometimes we struggle to reflect or really see our lives through the new eyes given to us at the moment of our salvation. We're like a person who has been wearing glasses her whole life and then gets LASIK surgery and suddenly sees 20/20. She suddenly notices mold in the corner of the shower that she never could see before and is amazed at what she observes when she dives in a pool and opens her eyes underwater. Then, out of habit, she reaches for her glasses and puts them on, opening her eyes in confusion as things appear blurred and distorted through her lenses.

Old habits can be hard to break, and old ways of seeing things, even harder to change. How were you taught to process your faith growing up? What were you taught were acceptable, and perhaps mandatory, ways to connect with God? Have you reevaluated what you've learned in light of your own study of God's Word? Or have you simply clung to what you were taught because the thought of reexamining your faith sounds tiring?

Taking the time to engage our faith and then process our faith is well worth it.

Having faith is hard at times. Obedience is even harder. I'm a person who wears his heart on his sleeve. I'm also a person who genuinely cares about and likes just about anyone. I go out of my way to make people feel comfortable and a part of a group or setting. For the leadership gurus out there, WOO (winning others over) is in my top five strengths. At the same time, I'm also a person who grew up with more than his fair share of hurt, disappointment, and anxiety as a result of my diagnosis, because society says that's what happens to people like me. Ironically, because of the way I'm wired, I see God everywhere in everything, but there are still times I feel like he is not there or has abandoned me. My mind and heart know he's there, but somehow in my soul I feel conflicted. I'm unsure what my spiritual walk will be like in a week, let alone ten years from now; but one thing I do know is that God is real.

Framing our faith is about getting down to the nitty-gritty. It's about getting dirty—not just a little bit of dirt on your knees but immersing ourselves into the process of hard work, the critical work. It's going back to the routines and practices we know God uses to speak to us. And it's about looking for and creating opportunities to connect with him. It's sitting back and praying simple, honest prayers to know his will because we know he is listening, even on the days when we question his presence.

I struggled with this. Heck, I still do. I remember when I got a call from a major network a year into ministry. It was all out of the blue. Though to be honest, I was also going through a tough time, and there was excitement that this could be the start of something new. Long story short, they knew that I left television and wanted me to think about heading up a section of their news operation. At the same time, I got another call from a twenty-four-hour news network. Both positions were really enticing: the money was great, the benefits were perfect, and the cities were awesome. I formally interviewed for both positions. My wife and I prayed. Job offers were extended, but something didn't feel right. We continued to pray and wrestle with the decision, looking at every opportunity from every angle. And then one Sunday morning, God gave me my answer.

There I was, sitting in the same seat I sat in every Sunday, when all the sudden I realized what was going on. God spoke, and I listened. He revealed to me that when I had left television, I had surrendered 99 percent of my heart to him and his call on my life, but I had been holding back 1 percent just in case I failed miserably. I had a backup plan. I wanted to know that if it all fell apart I would have something to return to—something I knew I could succeed in doing. So God did what any father would do for his son: he provided great opportunities and provision, but he was going to show me what it was really like. (I need to stop and add a disclaimer here, because I have a lot of friends in the television industry and I have incredibly fond memories of my time there. God used the relationships I made there and the experiences I had to shape my life and enrich it in ways that have forever impacted me.)

God reminded me of my time in the television industry, how when it was good it was incredibly good, but when it was bad, man, was it bad. He began to wreck me right there in my comfortable spot during worship. God wanted me to have faith in the direction he had called me; he also wanted me to be faithful no matter how tough or hard things might get. I had a sight problem—I had been only hesitantly trusting God, and I needed to fully surrender my heart to him. I had processed my decision in light of the facts, but I had been waiting to see it from God's perspective, knowing that he could see my life in its entirety, and not just from the narrow, close-up view that I had. God patiently let me process the decision on my own, waiting for me to ask him for his thoughts. And then in a moment when he knew my heart was open and I was ready to listen, he took my hand that Sunday morning and showed me his will. I took his advice, and I turned down those tempting opportunities. Looking back it was one of the best, most freeing, and terrifying decisions I have ever made. I wouldn't change it for a thing.

What a graceful, patient God we have who will let us wonder and question, struggle and fight, pursue and seek, all the while never leaving our side, never getting angry with us, just waiting for the moment when we are ready to listen and then revealing truth to us in ways we can understand. And then we come to realize that indeed, God's thoughts are higher than our thoughts and his ways higher our ways.[4] Even our best thoughts and ideas are "low" thinking[5] in comparison to his incredible wisdom. We need God to show us the light.

SEEK AND YOU WILL SEE

Paul prayed that believers would be able to focus, that "the eyes of [our] heart[s]" would be "enlightened."[6] He prayed we would be able to "see" all of God's beauty and glory and become arrested by it, impacted by it, and filled up with it! This is an incredibly passionate prayer. His powerful prayer continued as he asked that we would be "able to comprehend"[7] the incredible expanse of God's love in Christ. To see the breadth, width, height, and length of this great love. That we may gain a panoramic, or wide-angle, perspective of the infinitely powerful love of God and that it would fill us. When we invite Jesus into our lives and into our processing of life, our Savior never turns down an invitation.

One of my favorite stories in the Bible is where the two

disciples are walking on the road to Emmaus right after Jesus was crucified. They were feeling deeply sad and talking together about what had happened, trying to make sense of it all. Suddenly, Jesus appeared and joined the disciples walking along with them, but they didn't recognize him.[8]

"What are these things you are talking about while you walk?" Jesus asked them.[9]

One of the disciples responded, telling him about how Jesus had been sentenced to death, crucified and buried and how some women had gone to his tomb to only find the tomb empty. They had heard other people say Jesus was alive, the disciples told their traveling companion, but they had not seen him.[10] Jesus then told them, "You are foolish and slow to believe everything the prophets said."[11]

As they reached Emmaus, the disciples invited Jesus to stay with them. When they sat down at the table to eat, Jesus took the bread and gave thanks, broke it, and gave it to them. Immediately, the disciples' eyes were opened, and they saw that it was Jesus.[12]

I love to imagine myself as one of those disciples. I think of the half-smile Jesus must have been hiding as he listened to these men process out loud who they believed he was and what had happened to him. And ever so patiently, Jesus walked them through the Scriptures and showed them who he was and God's plan for sending him to earth. Jesus never shut the guys up, telling them how dumb they were for not seeing the obvious or laughing at them for their questions or ponderings. He loved them. He loved their questions. He loved their struggles. Because it showed that these men really cared and passionately wanted to know and understand their Father. And God will always show himself to people who are seeking him.

Taking time to reflect and process allows us to focus and see what God has placed right in front of us; it creates a time of spiritual vision and restoration. Reengaging our faith energizes us on the inside and gives a spark of life to a spiritual relationship that may feel tired. And God is faithful to show himself to whoever seeks him. He is a creative God, and he reveals himself to us in creative ways. He speaks to us where we are and in a language we understand. He is with us in our times of joy and in our moments of darkness. He is our ever-present, all-knowing, always-loving Savior, God, and friend.

ELEVEN

DARKNESS

*Deep into that darkness peering, long I stood there,
wondering, fearing, doubting, dreaming dreams no
mortal ever dared to dream before.*

—EDGAR ALLAN POE

E very time we take a picture, we capture a moment in
time. Some photographs make statements while others
ask questions. Some trigger memories about the past
while others inspire excitement about the future. Some are clear
and defined in their meaning while others are more fluid in
their interpretation.

Regardless, a photograph has a way of revealing truth—a
truth about something that has happened in our lives. Good
photographs are seen long before they happen. They are visualized in the mind before the shutter is triggered. They are brought

to life and made in the darkness. A photographer is constantly aware of the tiny details in a person's life that reveal greater truths.

DARKNESS, LIGHT, AND PEACE

It was early November in Paris, and a frozen layer of precipitation hung over the city wistfully as darkness spread down the Champs-Élysées. I stood at the foot of the Arc de Triomphe as darkness shrouded the city. As I looked up to admire this towering linchpin of the historic axis, a faint, gentle light broke through the gauze and illuminated one side of the Arc. I quickly reached for my camera, even though I knew I could not remake the perfection and beauty that nature was creating before me. My finger stayed posed over the shutter release, my eye glued to the viewfinder. As the sky and my surroundings went completely black, one subtle yet sharp beam of light hit La Paix de 1815. I looked closely . . . and clicked the shutter.

In that moment, I saw an epic battle between darkness and light being played out by nature over this monument that, for years, has been a rallying point of French troops after successful military campaigns. The mood was pensive as the emotions focused on the past. I wanted to move beyond a trite interpretation of darkness to let the image speak to me metaphorically. When people looked at this photo, I wanted them to be able to feel the subtle warmth of the darkness and how the gentle illumination of the word *La Paix* admits that darkness exists. I would find out later that *La Paix* translates to "peace," and hidden amid the darkness of this photo was a ceremony being held below by the people of France in commemoration of the anniversary of the armistice between France and Germany in 1918, ending World War I.

The image reveals a bold, solitary structure that seems alone in the darkness as delicate light brings to life a relief from its marble side. The darkness frames this construction with comfort, just as a mother would cradle her ailing son, while the aggressive illumination of its facade reveals detailed craftsmanship and represents the warring masculinity of the father. The intertwining of darkness and light creates a sense of peace.

DON'T BE AFRAID OF THE DARK

One of the first lessons new photographers are taught is to make sure their images have a sufficient amount of light. Without proper lighting, the subjects will be lost. And as young children, one of our greatest desires is to stay in the light. Children crave the ability to fully see what is around them and are terrified of things hidden in the darkness. Without light, they feel lost and alone. Yet as both photographers and children grow and mature, they realize that the darkness is not something to fear, but rather to master.

As parents, we reassure our children, "There's no need to be afraid of the dark." We would be wise to take our own advice.

Our paths have not always been clear. Our journeys have been far from easy. Our walks have been dark at times. The darkness of our lives never really gets any good press. We mention it as if it's a four-letter word. It's as if we want our dark places trapped away in the void underneath our stairs or lost, so that only our backspace key knows all our secrets. We do this because darkness is void. Darkness is risky, silent, scary, evil, chaotic, and unknown. It's uncertain. Darkness causes us to search. Darkness reveals our vulnerability and weaknesses. Our dark moments are something we're hesitant to share with even our dearest friends, let alone complete strangers.

But we must not fear the dark.

In addition to revealing truth, a photograph has a way of relating truth. We hope the viewer subconsciously says, "I may not know what is in your shadows, but I can relate because I know what is in my own shadows. I can connect because I find myself with the contrasts that life's contradictions create."

I have spent my life telling stories to move an audience to take action, whether it's to inform, evoke emotion, or make a purchase. The truths found in these stories are buried deep down, beyond the surface and many times, layered in the shadows. A good photographer does not shun darkness but discovers how best to use it to his or her advantage in telling the story.

YOU: UNEDITED

As a photographer, I live a life of light and dark. These opposing forces hold my work and our world together. They are the dualities of complementary forces, like yin and yang. By definition, yin is negative, dark, and feminine, while yang is positive, bright, and masculine, and their interaction is thought to maintain the harmony of the universe and to influence everything within it.[1] There are yin and yang aspects in everything because light could not be appreciated if darkness didn't exist; without light, shadow cannot exist. For instance, if you shoot a photo that is overexposed, in the edit you need to pull in shadows to create contrast. The same thing goes for our stories—if we share only the parts of our story that shine and are bright, our story has far less of an impact. Perfection is much more difficult to relate to.

The best stories are those of ordinary people who have found truth in their imperfection. Their stories are messy, off-color, and not safe. Their stories are not perfect by any stretch of the imagination, but they reveal a faith with teeth, a faith that can penetrate dysfunction, and a level of authenticity that inspires.

Too many times, once we move from a non-Christian view to a Christian view, we put on airs that proclaim, "I'm saved and just because of that, life is peachy." That's far from the truth. Yet why on a daily basis do we skip to the end of our stories and omit the gritty, not-so-nice details? The moment we skip to the end of our stories, we fall captive to the stories of this world, we lose the uniqueness of our story, and in turn we lose the power of the gospel to be light in real darkness.[2]

I firmly believe God has designed us to share our whole stories, stories that include both extremely transformative and disgustingly dark moments. In sharing the entire narrative of our lives, we act in surrender—surrendering to the actual story that God himself has woven through our imperfect, sometimes dysfunctional lives, rather than trying to force God to edit out chunks of his work in order to achieve a G rating.

Darkness is heavy with meaning, ripe with history, and laden with emotion. In it, we find pain, vulnerability, and something deeply true that communicates far more than any written word could. I learned very early in my career that getting to this place with my subjects really allowed their souls to shine.

It's a place to which many don't go. A place many people won't let others into because they are ashamed—still hurt, still grieving. But it is also a place of beauty and healing, and ultimately, it is the keeper of the truth. As we move about our lives, most of us have adopted an eyes-wide-shut and muffled-ears policy when it comes to communicating outside our comfort zones.

We fear that letting someone into our darkest of places lends itself to exposing our vulnerabilities. Or that if we peer into someone else's darkness, we might be frightened by what we see.

We are afraid of the darkness in our own stories and the stories of others. No story is all light. The photo editing software we use today has trained us to filter out the imperfections of what we capture. But there are moments when those imperfections, those errors, and those stains add richness and help us tell the story more fully. As philosopher Francis Bacon says, "In order for the light to shine so brightly, the darkness must be present."[3]

But we run a risk. What if in our initial excitement to capture others' stories, we find things unexpected?

What if we . . .

- focus our lens onto a single mom who has come to Christ, only to find in her shadows that she has moved in with her boyfriend and still hasn't fully weaned herself off of pot?

- capture the image of a young couple who has been giving to their church and are experiencing financial growth, only to hear them share how God has really been blessing them at the local casino's blackjack tables?
- film the testimony of a kid in youth group who led his friend to the Lord . . . as they were sitting next to each other in detention for getting caught smoking in the school bathrooms?

We are worried that some real-life details in our stories might undermine our doctrines, unwrite our core values, and venture into heresy. Or that by giving these details their place in the composition, we are somehow glorifying them.

The discovery of darkness is not an endorsement of it. It is an acknowledgment that it exists and that we serve a God big enough to make beauty out of it.

In some ways, stripping our stories of life's sometimes messy details is what makes our faith seem so irrelevant to the dirty details of real life. Rather, we might learn from a movie producer who makes a film about atrocities committed against Jews during the Holocaust. Without pausing the movie to allow the director to "teach" the audience what he wants them to walk away with, he trusts the viewers are able to use their knowledge of the human condition to sort through what appears on the screen. And sure enough, the audience members don't leave the theater thinking Nazis have been exalted or believing racially inspired murders were glorified. They follow the nuances of each character's corruption and growth, and their minds naturally seek the teachable moments of light in the story.

WHAT GOOD IS A STORY WITHOUT CONFLICT?

Life is dysfunctional. We make choices that can have a positive or a negative impact on ourselves and on those around us. Those choices are great seedlings in our stories. Right or wrong, they reveal something about us, something God has created for a purpose. All great stories must have conflict, or the story cannot evolve. All great characters must have failures and tension, or they will not be able to grow.

The Bible says, "Where sin abounded, grace abounded much more."[4] Where darkness is present, light shines that much brighter. Without the recognition of sin, grace does not have an opportunity to save.

Without the flaws, the errors, the failings, the darkness in our stories, what story is there really to tell? The greatest story on earth is that of a humanity who failed and a great Savior who came to its rescue. Where is the glory of the rescue without the failing? Where is the scandalous outpouring of grace without the sin and brokenness?

When we buckle to fear and look past the bad thoughts we battle on a routine basis—our feelings of being rejected or being terrified of intimacy—it strips stories of their most real, powerful qualities. Ben Okri, a Nigerian poet and novelist, insists that storytelling hints at a fundamental human unease; it hints at human imperfection, so much so that where there is perfection, there is no story to tell.[5]

Perhaps the hardest part in all of this is that we have a hard time getting to these dark places of truth in our own lives. Carl Jung says, "Knowing your own darkness is the best method for dealing with the darkness of other people."[6]

REDEEMING THE DARK SPOTS

Great talents are lovely but also dangerous fruits on the tree of humanity.[7] And as an artist, I deal with a struggle, a clash between two paradigms. It's as if an invisible war is being waged. Just like in photography, I war against darkness and light. Internally, I'm involved in this cosmic conflict, while the rest of the world sees an image of someone who has everything buttoned up and going right. But on the inside, I'm battling struggles that no one knows but myself. Struggles that are there from the minute I wake up to the minute I go to sleep. We all are confronted by these internal conflicts, and often they are the most difficult battles we may face in life. Battles that no matter how hard we may fight, we feel we can never win.

I think this is the plight of an artist. The curse of an overactive and creative mind. The debt that must be paid for thinking and marching to the beat of a different drummer or attempting to hold onto my revolutionary beliefs while embracing the reality of Christianity.

I am not perfect.

I am broken, wrecked, and adrift.

The wars I waged were fraught with weaknesses, setbacks, and failures—not being accepted for who I was, and possessing a talent and passion that was misunderstood.

Most of our stories have many different conflicts. For my entire life I have been trying to defy those who have typecast me, like my first grade teacher who told my parents that I would never go to college. Then there were those who told me I had no talent, that my unique style of photography, painting, and writing didn't connect because it was too avant-garde, and that I pushed the limits of what is considered normal.

The plot piece of my story was that I was waging this battle between man versus man. It was me against the typecasting antagonists capable of defeating me like intelligent alien robots from the planet Cybertron. But more importantly, I was also engaged in an altercation with myself. I battled minor internal problems that at the time felt pretty major—questions of self-doubt like, "Why can't people see what I see?" "Am I really a misfit?" "Why would people say stuff to hurt me when I've done nothing to them?" "Am I broken?" "Will I amount to anything in life?"

Depressing, right? I was so negative that you could have put me in a darkroom and I would have developed. But as Mother Teresa says, "Words which do not give the light of Christ increase the darkness."[8] My hidden crusade got to the point that any time a choice was necessary, my mind filled with confusion, self-doubt, and second-guessing. The struggle I was dealing with was denial of my true self, thinking I was a social recluse and these conflicts were about much more important matters than anything else going on.

I dove into a battle to prove everyone wrong, but every time I proved someone wrong, the battles became harder; they never subsided. Each battle drained a little more out of me, and bit by bit I began to lose who I really was.

Our world coerces us into adopting abstract ideas or preconceived notions about how we should act, which often conflicts with our individual reality. We war against being unique and bask in the comfort of swimming in a sea of same.

It took me a while to see this darkness in my life, because I was willingly overlooking clear direction from God, choosing not to see his guidance through this time in my life. I was able to finally find strength in God by holding onto the truth he had shown me: to be me—to embrace my weaknesses and let him be shown strong through them. Now I realize that God is not only our authority, but he is also the author of our life's story—and as he writes these stories, he uses our past to reveal our future.

What darkness in your life have you been hiding, terrified that if someone were to find out, you'd be cast aside? How can bringing to the surface the dark places inside of you, allow the light of God to penetrate your soul, bringing you the warmth and love and reassurance that you so desperately need? Or how has God already redeemed some of the dark spots in your past and used them to enrich the story of your life?

Our God is the God who wastes nothing. Who redeems everything. Who makes beauty from ashes and gladness from mourning.[9] If you find yourself in a place where the darkness feels overwhelming, don't despair, because God will bring the light.

TWELVE

LIGHT

*I am sure—as sure as anyone can be of anything—that
in the end there will be light, an all-pervading insight
illuminating the immense structure of the cosmos,
revealing the rightful place and purpose of man.*

—ANDREAS FEININGER

What is a photograph but an attempt by a photographer to preserve an image that encompasses the splendor, illustriousness, and wonder of the moment it was captured? But there is one pivotal element that can either make or break a photograph. Light.

Simply put, light is the photographer's ultimate revealer, and photographers depend heavily on it. We are imbued with its essence—knowing it, expecting it, needing it. Without light, photographs would merely be shades of black silhouetted in gray. And so photographers chase it throughout the day, searching and seeking the perfect light to capture and store the perfect memories. The way it cascades across the landscape and the way it hits the chaff in fields of wheat at sunset. The way it cuts through the small crack of the door and makes its way across a dark room. Or the way light bends and refracts its glare on ice.

Light can be both powerful and precious, playful and priceless. Should someone attempt to photograph a moment and disregard the importance of light and its effect on the surroundings, they will have nothing to show for it outside of an overexposed, colorless glare or a flat, grainy mix of shadows with nothing truly visible.

One can't ignore the power of light in the realm of photography. It is the lifeblood of our industry. Who can deny it? I know I can't. Denying photographers light is like denying a fish water or a person air. We are utterly reliant upon it.

Light plays a huge role in nearly every aspect in my work as a photographer. The only way to create and take the perfect picture is to know the light and to know how to work with it.

There are certainly rules and guidelines to follow in order to use light to the best of its ability. Beyond simply observing its presence, you must understand and appreciate what a gift you have. Every time I place my eye to the viewfinder of a camera, preparing to snap a shot, I take a breath and recognize where the light is and how it will affect the shot I am trying to take.

To be a skilled photographer, one needs to understand and be constantly aware of the light as it moves across the sky or if it is honed by another source. And light can come in so many forms, sometimes appearing as a rising sun, peeking out from behind the clouds, or as the soft smolder of a fading firelight. Light can be the flickering glow of a fluorescent light bulb in an office building or the decorative lamp in the living room. Everywhere you look there is light; one need only look in the right places.

LIGHT AS A METAPHOR

With the knowledge and ability to hone and display light, I believe it is infinitely easier to understand and see the world. For me, light serves to highlight and show me the beauty and delight found in our world. It showcases the natural wonder in the wide-open landscapes of our vast and impressive earth.

But more than simply a source of visibility, light is a powerful tool of metaphor. It is the symbol of all that is good and right in the world. The rays of light from the sun are a shining reminder of the truth and beauty of a world created for peace. The everlasting glow of the sun, ever in motion, serves as a reminder that the good of the world can and will continue to exist and flourish. As Martin Luther King Jr. explains, "Darkness cannot drive out darkness: only light can do that. Hate cannot drive out hate: only love can do that."[1]

Without light the flowers and trees and all those wondrous living things would perish. The light serves as a guiding aura to follow and to appease. The shining symbol of goodness also casts shadows and creates shades of meaning in the world. Just as only light can distinguish and help us recognize that darkness exists, in this world there will always be darkness to make us aware of just how beautiful light is. Yet God promises us the light will always overcome it: "The Light shines in the darkness, and the darkness has not overpowered it."[2]

Hidden within these shades and subshades of shadow and light is the reality of the world. When the first light passed across the surface of the earth, it cast several individual rays of light and subsequently, illuminated the darkness. Each of these lights were their own identity, carrying with it a mission all its own. The first touches of light upon the earth awakened the life of the earth, rousing the landscape itself to the dawn of a new day. It is with this light that the world came to be what it is known as today.

As light hits the unseen shadows, it brings the distortions and the gloom into focus, allowing us to peel back the layers upon layers of lies and deceit the shadows try to hide. These layers are built up over time, constantly constructing thicker and denser layers to conceal the increasing number of trickeries and secrets. These shadows form on the lack of light—they fester where the eyes of humanity cannot see. But one single ray of light can work to penetrate those films and layers, revealing their secrets to the world.

And this light, which originates far away and removed from us here on earth, makes our lives possible, makes photography possible. Beyond the essentiality of light, it acts as both a beacon and a promise. Light is the guiding path; it illuminates the way. It is the one true element within a world on the verge of chaos. It brings order and helps us to remain faithful to this world we live in and the memory of how we came to be.

Light is the faithful. Light is the way. Light is here to save us from the darkness that threatens our world. Light is confidence. Light is holy and encompassing. Light is the one true way. Light is a promise of a new day. Light is eternal. Light is Jesus.

BROKEN PROMISES

This light that was bestowed upon the earth was sent as a promise. That just as the sun rises each morning, the light will continue to reveal all the darkness that lay hidden in the mysterious shades and shadows.

We all need light to guide our lives, for without it we would be lost. God places his light inside whoever chooses to open themselves up to his love and salvation. As followers of Jesus, we are filled with his light. And as people who crave the light, we'll be drawn not only to the light found in relationship with our Father, but also to his light shining in those around us. Poet Maya Angelou senses the light a person can bring to others: "You rose into my life like a promised sunrise, brightening my days with the light in your eyes."[3] But because these lights are housed in earthen vessels, sometimes our connections don't always work out the way we think they will.

Just as we trust that the sun will rise each day, we also trust that promises made to one another will be followed through on. But we all know from personal letdowns that those words are sometimes just that—words. Promises are easily broken, but only through difficulty can they be remedied.

This is a common tale we all share. We all make promises that we'll do something for someone, but regrettably don't follow through on what we had promised to do. The reverse is also true. Others have made promises to us, and in turn, they have broken those vows. There always seems to be an excuse for a broken promise—forgetting, being too busy, or sometimes just not wanting to do it. The promise of light shines through vessels that are cracked, damaged, and broken, and as a result, sometimes those pledges fall short of what the promisor intended.

We first experiment with breaking promises when we are young. My son, Noah, is a typical six-year-old, and he has promised his mom and me on several occasions that he won't sneak off to our bedroom to get the iPad that sits on my bedside table. He really likes to play Angry Birds, but he promised to leave the iPad alone as we'd asked. He pondered and he thought on his choices, but in the end his desire to play a silly game based on wingless birds outweighed his desire to keep his promise.

One night, as soon as we turned away, Noah ran upstairs and snagged the iPad. Quickly he made off with the electric joy, scurrying all the way back to his room where he hid under the covers on his bed. There he sat in his room, iPad in hand, ready to play the game. But as he began to play, somehow it wasn't as sweet and rewarding as he had expected it to be. The realization of the broken promise changed how he viewed the once so-desired device as he came and told his mother and me of his actions.

Those of us who are honest go into a promise with the full intention of keeping our pledge until the very end. But sometimes people change their minds and decide to break the promise. This is not to say that promises were meant to be broken or that promises were meant to be halfhearted undertakings. In general, people don't make promises they intend to break.

Promises are meant to be declarations that say, "I will make this happen" or, "I will definitely do this." Yet the sting of a broken promise is a pain we feel each time an oath, an assurance, or a guarantee is called off. Each and every time such a commitment is disregarded we feel it in our souls—like a piece of our souls is being chipped away, little by little, until there seems to be almost nothing left.

As time wears on and the constant chipping away of our confidence in others continues, we grow more jaded and cynical. We scoff at the declarations and vows made by others, believing they, too, will only let us down. We lose our faith in humanity.

It is ironic, then, that without faith in others we'll never be able to accept or receive promises that are made to us. If we ignore the bounty of the good faith and charity that lurks in all people, how will we ever see what is in store for us?

THE KINGDOM OF LIGHT

This reminds me of another story about Noah and promises—but this time it features the Noah of the Bible. You may have heard the story. To sum it up, the story was set in a time of great evil, and God saw that only one righteous man was left on the earth. That man was Noah. To rid the world of the evil and to start anew, God ordered Noah to build an ark. And Noah did.[4]

Then God ordered Noah to collect two of each animal (and seven pairs of the clean animals) and place them in the ark. And Noah did. When Noah and the animals were safely onboard, a great rainstorm came and flooded the earth, drowning everyone and everything not aboard the ark. But the animals and Noah were safe.[5]

The rain poured and poured until one day God made the sun come out and the rain stopped. God told Noah to stay aboard until he told him it was time to get off. And Noah did. He looked up and saw a great sign in the sky, a promise to the world that

God would never again flood the world. That promise came in the form of the first rainbow.[6]

God made promises to Noah, and he kept them. Noah made promises to God, and he kept them. Because Noah put his trust in God, even when the rest of the world around him was as untrustworthy as they come, Noah was able to hear God's voice clearly. Noah didn't let all the hurt and pain and cruelty inflicted upon him by others jade his heart toward God. God's light was able to penetrate Noah's soul because Noah refused to let the darkness around him close him off to God's voice. And that trust became his and his family's salvation.

God isn't human. He took on human form when he sent his Son, Jesus—but he is spirit and he is truth. We may feel let down when others don't keep their promises to us, but we can always put our faith and trust in God, knowing that he keeps his word.[7]

If my ability to make promises or trust in promises made to me were based upon how others keep their promises, there would be no escape from the shadows, the gloom, the distrust. The word of man is shifting sand. But if I can find a promise, simple and true, personal and deep, to anchor the way I see the world, then light begins to dispel darkness. I can trust again. I can hope anew. I can be free to see the world with new eyes.

TRANSFERRED TO THE KINGDOM OF LIGHT

We have been transferred from the kingdom of darkness—that kingdom of a thousand broken promises, of double-talk and double crossers, of uncertainty in whom we can really trust—and transferred to the kingdom of light, the kingdom of the promise kept, of eternal longevity and security in the One who can be trusted. We can live and promise and serve and love and see differently because he brought us a promise that will never be broken.

His promise is light because it reveals the truest nature, intent, and will of God—to save us to the uttermost. To spare nothing in his promise to secure us eternally. I can see his plan more clearly and I can see his instruction more clearly because I believe in that promise.

Light is important to a panorama because without it we can't see. Promise is important to our life panorama, because without it, the light of hope dims. I see less clearly because my hope is waning. But in Christ, light floods our heart and eyes because we clearly see the One who makes the promise. And we see more clearly when we trust more deeply. We are children of light because we live in a promise that God made with himself that he will honor for all of eternity.[8] As Paul says, "For all the promises of God in Him [Jesus] are Yes, and in Him Amen, to the glory of God through us."[9] David sang a song of thankfulness to God: "He will keep his agreement forever; he will keep his promises always."[10]

A distrustful person looks down, is closed off, and sees things through eyes squinted by skepticism. A hopeful person looks up with a heart unguarded and eyes open, searching for truth and love. Trust opens our heart, brings down our guard, and allows us to see more clearly. The more deeply we trust in God's promises to us, the more we truly believe that he is who he says he is and that he will do for us what he said he will do.[11] Then we can relax the tightness of distrust in our souls and begin to let God's light pour in and warm that which the lies of others have made cold.

We must remember that "God is not a human being, and he will not lie. He is not a human, and he does not change his mind. What he says he will do, he does. What he promises, he makes come true."[12] Sometimes we try to understand God by filtering him through our experiences of others, but God is not fallible like us. People will break their promises to us, but God will not. When we try to understand God by filtering him through our human perspective, we do him a disservice and we do ourselves a disservice.

Saint Augustine urges us that when people choose to withdraw "far from a fire, the fire continues to give warmth, but they grow cold. When people choose to withdraw far from light, the light continues to be bright in itself but they are in darkness. This is also the case when people withdraw from God."[13]

FAITH THAT LIGHT EXISTS IN THE DARKNESS

To believe that God is worthy to be trusted, we must have faith. There will be times when our lives are as dark as a cloudy, moonless night, where we can't see our hands in front of our faces. In those moments we will have the opportunity to decide whether we believe that God's light still exists or not. Will we let what we see with our physical eyes determine what we believe in our souls? Will we let our emotional cries drown out the gentle voice of his Spirit? Can we, like Noah, trust in God when the storms rage, the boat is rocking, and the floodwaters cover everything in sight? Or can we believe that above the layers of raging skies is a sun that still shines as bright as ever, that at any moment will break through the clouds and begin to warm that which has been drenched in pain and sadness?

As a photographer, I have learned to search for light, because it is always present in some form. On a cloudy day, I can still see a gentle glow pushing through. On a dark evening, I can look up and see the stars. On the blackest night, I can use a flash to make light of my own.

And God's light is always present in our lives in some form. One of God's greatest promises is that he will never leave us or forsake us.[14] He is always there. On cloudy days, his light gently glows. On dark evenings, his light reflects. On the blackest night, he has placed his light inside of us—his Spirit is light that illuminates our souls from within. We are never without his love and his light.

The darkness around us never, ever changes the truth that the sun exists. And the darkness around us never, ever changes the truth that the Light exists. Jesus said of himself, "I am the light of the world. He who follows Me shall not walk in darkness, but have the light of life."[15] Jesus is faithful. Jesus can be trusted. Jesus is the Light.

LIVING IN THE LIGHT

God wants us to see the love he has for us, to know it is there and make the decision to accept it. His care is genuine and real, and he has undoubtedly declared that love for us—all we need to do is open our hearts to him. This distinct mark[16] of love from our Father is a commission, a command, a beacon of light to the world. It's a powerful proclamation that Jesus is the light of the world and amazingly so are we.[17] As his children we have been created not for his infinite joy and glorification, but to share it. All our lights shine brighter when we pass them along. And in the very nature of light and its shine, it's our responsibility to do everything we can to make our light as bright as possible. We were created to walk in the light. We were created to reflect the light.

As his children, God has placed his light within each and every one of us. His greatest hope for us is that we would allow ourselves to be filled with his love so that we may reflect that light into our everyday lives. Just as light reflects off an object being photographed, we are God's exposure. And the light we project shines a warm glow of God's love on to a world darkened by sin and sadness.

In a world of broken vows, may we be the promise keepers. In a land of falsehoods, may we be voices of truth. In a sea of sadness, may we be beacons of hope. May we help bring the kingdom of God here, to earth. May we carry out God's restorative work of creation among us. May we help others see the joy there is to be found in living in the Light. And as we go about doing the work of God that he created us to do, may our faith be enriched and made stronger and be framed into a faith that is uniquely ours, making us uniquely *his*.

AFTERWORD

BY BEN ARMENT

The best artists and storytellers have the same world around them as the rest of us. It's the same viewfinder, the same easel, the same software, and the same subjects. There is no special access to great art.

But there is a way of seeing the world that differs. Ira Glass once said, "The best stories happen to those who can tell them."[1] He might as well have said, "The best photos happen to those who can see them." The moments do not differ, only the eyes.

This reminds me of what Jesus told the throng who surrounded him in hopes of a miracle: "You have eyes, but you don't really see. You have ears, but you don't really listen."[2] He feared that a limited perspective was keeping them from seeing his kingdom around them.

I don't know about you, but I want to be one of those who *sees*. And this requires sabotaging my *other* way of seeing the world—the one that is limited by my physical vantage point, my propped-up schedule, and my subjective priorities.

After all, our eyes are not the only way we can see.

Years ago, when my oldest son was a baby, my wife and I ran into a friend at church named Alex, who is blind. After a bit of small talk, Alex was kind enough to address our child, who was nestled in my arms.

But because Alex couldn't see, he assumed my son was standing. So he knelt down to say hello, which happened to be the height of my kneecaps. At first, I didn't know what to do. I didn't want to embarrass him. So I quickly knelt down too with Wyatt in my arms and guided Alex's hand toward my son's face, so he could feel how small he was.

Feeling those tiny cheeks, ears, and nose with his fingertips, Alex realized there was no need for him to be crouched down. So he slowly rose to a standing position. His new perspective changed his posture. Suddenly, he could *see* my son.

The secret to experiencing great stories and taking great photographs is the same as having great faith. It is to be one who *sees*. It is to sabotage your *other* way of seeing the world so you can see a new reality. And when you do this, it will change your posture.

I run a creative summit in Chicago each year called STORY. More than one thousand creators, dreamers, and entrepreneurs come together to be inspired, learn from experts, and connect with each other. These are people who see amazing moments and tell captivating stories.

One of the things that surprises me most about these

gatherings is how misunderstood the seeing community is. They don't measure the world with spreadsheets, profit margins, and sales quotas. So they appear irrational, impractical, and even naive to everyone else. Their decisions don't seem logical because they're not based on a conventional way of seeing.

This community has learned to cope with the stigma of being seen as outcasts by consoling themselves at creative meet-ups, as if they were recovery groups, and on social media, where other artists validate their profession. They keep their heads down at work, pulling all-nighters and doing whatever it takes to justify their employment. The ambitious ones open up their own shops where they charge for their services like a band of soothsayers.

As a community organizer, my job is to encourage them to stick with their craft, to never give up, and to find meaning in their work. Staying true to this new perspective is worth it. Without these artists, the world would be a much less inspiring place. My hope is that the number of those who "see" will continue to grow. After all, with this gift comes an incredible calling.

———

In Exodus 35, God instructed the Israelites to build a tabernacle in the wilderness. This was a project intended for the priests but also for the artists.

The artist who was called upon to craft the materials in the sanctuary, including statues of angels, was a young man by the name of Bezalel of the tribe of Judah.[3] He was the grandson of Hur, the man who held up Moses' frail arms in battle.

The Israelites needed someone who could imagine what

angels looked like, and Bezalel was apparently someone who did. He saw the world differently. He came from a long line of important people like heads of state, yet he devoted his life to creating beautiful art. His backyard was probably strewn with gangly statues discarded from failed attempts.

But Bezalel kept at it, working hard and perfecting his craft. I'm sure his mother nagged him to find suitable employment to support a family. His father probably wondered why he couldn't be more like his brothers. And his grandfather probably grew frustrated at trying to show him how to throw a javelin.

But at the right moment, Bezalel was called upon as the only one who could depict the spiritual realm. He was commissioned to bring his unique vision to life in the very structure that housed God's presence. Thanks to Bezalel, the Israelites could actually see what a heavenly creature might look like. And it changed their posture.

———

The thing most people don't understand about artists, as well as those who see the kingdom of God all around them, is that they can't help but express what they've seen.

When the followers of Jesus, who were left behind after his death and resurrection, were told to keep their mouths shut, they responded, "We cannot keep quiet. We must speak about what we have seen and heard."[4]

This is who we are—people who have seen and heard and cannot help but recreate it.

Remember that your calling is a holy one. There is no difference between the priests and the artists anymore. When the temple veil was rent from top to bottom at Jesus' resurrection, it not only allowed the artists to enter the presence of God but it allowed the priests to roam the streets. Jesus made the two roles indistinguishable.

You are not only artist. You are priest.

NOTES

FOREWORD

1. From the documentary film *Mies van der Rohe*, directed by Georgia van der Rohe, sponsored by Knoll International and Zweites Deutsches Fernsehen, Mainz, produced by IFAGE Filmproduktion, Wiesbaden; English version, 1979.
2. Brian Greene, *The Elegant Universe: Superstrings, Hidden Dimensions, and the Quest for the Ultimate Theory* (New York: Norton, 1999).
3. "The Question Concerning Technology," first published in 1954, as found in *Martin Heidegger: Basic Writings*, rev. ed., ed. David Farrell Krell (San Francisco: Harper, 2008), 307–341.
4. Hans Urs von Balthasar, *Word and Revelation*, trans. A. V. Littledale (New York: Herder and Herder, 1964), 162.
5. "The world will be redeemed by beauty." Fyodor Dostoevsky, *The Idiot*, trans. David Margarschack. (London: Penguin, 1986), 103. See the commentary on this statement by John W. DeGruchy, *Christianity, Art and Transformation: Theological Aesthetics in the Struggle for Justice* (Cambridge: Cambridge University Press, 2001), 97–102.
6. Brian Zahnd, *Beauty Will Save the World: Rediscovering the Allure and Mystery of Christianity* (Lake Mary, FL: Charisma House, 2012).
7. Yehudi Menuhin, *Unfinished Journey* (New York: Random House, 1979).

8. Rev. 19:10.
9. Ps. 29:2 NKJV.

INTRODUCTION

1. Steve Simon, *The Passionate Photographer: Ten Steps Toward Becoming Great* (Berkeley: Pearson Education, 2011), 31.

CHAPTER 2: ATTENTION

1. Stephen Marche, "Is Facebook Making Us Lonely?" *The Atlantic,* April 2, 2012, http://www.theatlantic.com/magazine/archive /2012/05/is-facebook-making-us-lonely/30893.
2. Paulo Coelho, *The Alchemist* (HarperCollins, 2007), 10.
3. Exod. 20:18–21.

CHAPTER 3: PURPOSE

1. Kenneth Burke, *Language as Symbolic Action: Essays on Life, Literature, and Method* (University of California Press, 1966),492.
2. Robert McKee, *Story: Style, Structure, Substance, and the Principles of Screenwriting* (New York: HarperCollins, 2010), 27.
3. Seth Godin, "The Forever Recession (and the coming revolution)," *Seth Godin* (blog), September 29, 2011, http://sethgodin.typepad .com/seths_blog/2011/09/the-forever-recession.html.
4. Gen. 2:18.
5. Josh. 4:7.
6. Michael F. Steltenkamp, *Nicholas Black Elk: Medicine Man, Missionary, Mystic* (Norman: University of Oklahoma Press, 2009), 14.
7. Jerome Rothenberg, *Technicians of the Sacred: A Range of Poetries from Africa, America, Asia, Europe & Oceania* (Berkeley: University of California Press, 1985), 546.

CHAPTER 4: PERFECTION

1. Jill W. Iscol and J. Peter W. Cookson, Jr., *Hearts on Fire: Twelve Stories of Today's Visionaries Igniting Idealism into Action* (New York: Random House, 2013), 138.

2. Gen. 18:9–15.

3. 2 Sam 11–12:14.

4. 1 Sam 13:13–14.

5. Anne Lamott, *Bird by Bird: Some Instructions on Writing and Life* (Random House: First Anchor Books, 1994), 28.

CHAPTER 5: LISTENING

1. David Ritz, "Inside Interviewing," *The Writer,* vol. 106, issue 3, March 1993, 15.

2. Ed Grimley is a fictional excessively cowlicked, hyperactive man who is obsessed with popular culture. He is a character created and portrayed by Martin Short during his time at Second City comedy troupe and later on *Saturday Night Live* in the 1980s.

3. Prov. 18:13.

4. Prov. 19:27.

5. James 1:19.

6. Luke 10:41–42.

7. 1 Sam. 3:10.

8. 1 Cor. 1:4–9.

CHAPTER 6: MOMENT

1. Edward Conney Lathem, *Interviews with Robert Frost* (St. Louis: Holt, Rinehart and Winston, 1966), 102.

2. Matt Knisely, "Chasing Sunsets: Austin, Texas," *Matt Knisely* (blog), April 7, 2013, http://mattknisely.com/blog/creativity/photography/chasing-sunsets/.

3. Ash Amin and Joanne Roberts, eds., *Community, Economic Creativity, and Organization* (New York: Oxford University Press, 2008), 95.

4. Newman Ivey White and Wayland D. Hand, eds., *The Frank C. Brown Collection of NC Folklore: Vol. VII: Popular Beliefs and Superstitions from North Carolina* (Durham: Duke University Press, 1977), 228.

5. Gen. 1:3–5.

6. Matt. 16:2–3 NIV.

7. Ps. 90:12 NKJV.

CHAPTER 7: PERSPECTIVE

1. *Groundhog Day* is a 1993 American comedy film starring Bill Murray and Andie MacDowell in which Murray's character relives the same day over and over again.
2. Col. 3:2.
3. Catherine M. Wallace, "Seven Don'ts Every Parent Should Do," *U.S. Catholic,* vol. 66, no. 1 (January 2001): 38–41. (http://www.catherinemwallace.com/Home/essays/seven-donts-every-parent-should-do)
4. Matt. 10:29–31.
5. Mark 1:40–45.
6. Rom. 11:25–26.
7. Rom. 11:28.
8. Daniel Taylor, *The Healing Power of Stories: Creating Yourself Through the Stories of Your Life* (New York: Doubleday, 1996), 69.

CHAPTER 8: SUBJECT

1. Chase Jarvis, *The Best Camera Is the One That's with You: iPhone Photography* (Berkeley: New Riders, 2010).
2. Tim Mantoani, *Behind Photographs: Archiving Photographic Legends* (San Diego: Channel Photographics, 2011), 18.
3. Buddy Media, "Strategies for Effective Wall Posts: A Timeline Analysis," http://www.slideshare.net/chrisrawlinson/buddymedia-strategies-for-effective-facebook-wall-posts.
4. Ansel Adams, "A Personal Credo, 1943," *American Annual of Photography,* vol. 58 (American Photographic Publis, 1948), 16.
5. Peter Cowie, *A Ribbon of Dreams: The Cinema of Orson Welles.* (South Brunswick and New York: A.S. Barnes and Company, 1973).
6. Edward Steichen, "Art: To Catch the Instant," *Time,* vol. 77, no. 15, April 7, 1961, 71.
7. Francis Bacon, http://www.photoquotes.com/showquotes.aspx?id=33.
8. Acts 22:6–11.
9. Acts 9:1–9.
10. Acts 26:9–11.
11. Acts 22:8–10.

12. Acts 13:9, Acts 22:10–13.
13. Acts 22:15.
14. Numbers 15:38–41.
15. Gen. 1:27.
16. Gen. 1:31 NKJV.

CHAPTER 9: COMPOSITION

1. William Shakespeare and Laura Jewry Valentine, *The Works of William Shakespeare* (New York: Frederick Warne & Company, 1873), 605.
2. William L. Pressly, *The Artist as Original Genius: Shakespeare's "Fine Frenzy" in Late-eighteenth-century British Art* (Associated University Press, 2007), 26.
3. Rom. 8:14–16.
4. Saint Augustine of Hippo, *Saint Augustine's Confessions: Works of Saint Augustine* (Sovereign Grace Publishers, 2001), 1.
5. D.I.A. Clines, "The Image of God in Man," Tyndale Bulletin 19 (1968), 101.
6. Eph. 2:10.
7. Gal. 3:26–28.
8. Marcel Proust, *In Search of Lost Time, The Captive, The Fugitive,* vol. 5. (New York: Random House Publishing Group 2013), 343.
9. Phil. 2:13.

CHAPTER 10: PROCESSING

1. Robert F. Bennett, Kurt Hanks, and Gerreld L. Pulsipher, *Gaining Control: Your Key to Freedom and Success* (Washington D.C.: Pocket Books, 1989), 6.
2. Jer. 29:13.
3. Ps. 1:2–3 NKJV.
4. Isa. 55:9.
5. Ps. 123:1.
6. Eph. 1:18 NIV.
7. Eph. 3:18 NKJV.
8. Luke 24:13–16.

9. Luke 24:17.
10. Luke 24:24–25.
11. Luke 24:25.
12. Luke 24:28–31.

CHAPTER 11: DARKNESS

1. *Merriam Webster's Collegiate Dictionary*, 11th ed., s.vv. "yin," "yang."
2. Matt Knisely, "God & Story," *Matt Knisely* (blog), April 7, 2013, http://mattknisely.com/blog/leadership/god-story/.
3. Francis Bacon, quoted in Darrell Griffin, *Business with a Purpose: Starting, Building, Managing and Protecting Your New Business* (Parker: Outskirts Press, 2010), 26.
4. Rom. 5:20 NKJV.
5. Ben Okri, *Birds of Heaven* (London: Phoenix Books, 1996), 22.
6. Carl Gustav Jung, *Letters* (Princeton: Princeton University Press, 1973), 237.
7. Carl Gustav Jung, *Psychological Reflections: An Anthology of the Writings of C.G. Jung, Volume 31 of Bollingen series* (Harper, 1961), 186.
8. Malcolm Muggeridge, *Something Beautiful for God: The Classic Account of Mother Teresa's Journey into Compassion* (New York: Harper & Row, 1971), 66.
9. Isa. 61:3 NKJV.

CHAPTER 12: LIGHT

1. Martin Luther King Jr., *Strength to Love* (Minneapolis: Fortress Press, 1977), 53.
2. John 1:5.
3. Maya Angelou, *The Complete Collected Poems of Maya Angelou* (New York: Random House, 2009), 128.
4. Gen. 6.
5. Gen. 7.
6. Gen. 9:11–17.
7. Psalms 57:10.
8. Heb. 6:13.
9. 2 Cor. 1:20 NKJV.

10. 1 Chron. 16:15.
11. A.W. Tozer, A.W. Tozer Bibile–KJV (Hendrickson Publishers, 2012), 1428.
12. Num. 23:19.
13. Maria Boulding, Boniface Ramsey, et al., *Expositions of the Psalms 99–120* (New York: New City Press, 2003), 168.
14. Heb. 13:5.
15. John 8:12 NKJV.
16. Eph. 1:13.
17. Matt. 5:14–16.

AFTERWORD

1. Ira Glass, quoted in "Long-Form Storytelling in a Short-Attention-Span World," *Frontline*, Public Broadcasting Service (PBS), March 17, 2011, http://www.pbs.org/wgbh/pages/frontline/2011/03/long-form-storytelling-in-a-short-attention-span-world.html.
2. Mark 8:18.
3. Exod. 31:1–8.
4. Acts 4:20.

ACKNOWLEDGMENTS

Writing is far from a solitary endeavor. Bringing a book to life from idea to pixels and finally pages takes a village, just as there are many who have taken part in my life's story, and it has been an adventure filled with amusement. During the deliberate, and often interrupted, transformation of this book, I have been lucky to accumulate many debts, only a few of which I have space to acknowledge here.

First and foremost, God. Thank you for being a God of divine and decisive moments who teaches us to let the events in our lives guide us to and through the exact things we need to discover.

Dana, my wife, my love, and my lobster, thank you for supporting all of my creative and contemplative passions with such enthusiasm and care. I am deeply blessed by your love for me and for our children; your selflessness and beauty remain undiminished. Lou-Lou and No-No, thank you for letting me see creativity and beauty with a new lens. You both are going to do great things for this world.

I benefited enormously from Blair and Don Jacobson, who saw the beauty that I see, and Matt Baugher, for immediately seeing something special, being personally touched by this text, giving me the opportunity and creative freedom to write from my heart, and allowing me to do it in my own way. Leonard Sweet, for your works, talks, and our relationship. Through them you have shown me how to live a life with grand passion and to be present in the moments our Father created. Stephanie Gutierrez and Adria Haley for amplifying this book through your gift and sharp critiques. You are awesome editors that challenged me to go after inspiration with a billy club. Nathan Davis, my wise guide, friend, card boy, and brother, for your deep belief and care for my soul. Ben Arment, for not only being a dear friend but for creating an environment such as STORY Chicago, where this book was conceived amid the dimly lit recesses. Greg and Denise Erway, for being answers to long lost prayers.

Most of all, I want to thank my parents and endless encouragers, Nancy and Terry Knisely (aka Mom and Dad), for always believing in me. Nothing fills my heart with more drive than hearing you say that you are proud of me. And Gary and Wilma Davidson, my in-laws, your unwavering support and care is the reason all of this was possible. Jointly, the affection you show for living life is what has inspired me to be passionate in everything I do. This book is every bit as much your accomplishment as it is mine. I love you.

I would like to extend a very special thank you to Rhett Smith for going before me and paving the way. And Sarah Cunningham, John Sowers, and Preston Morrison—thank you for being my early audience and encouraging me to press forward.

I am deeply grateful to my Pastor Robert Morris, Michael Buckingham, Tiffany Humphrey, David Lermy, Chris Martin, Jamie and Jen Austin, Trey Hill, Austin Mann, Esther Havens, Kyle Steed, Ginger Worthington Casebeer, Alece Ronzino, Katie

Moon, Gina Calvert, Kim and Andy Bohon, Curtis Simmons, Robin Jones, Jeff Hook, Mark Anderson, Doug Legore, Ted Canova, Dave Wertheimer, Patrick Dodd, Andrejs Dabars, Rick Gray, Blake Edgmond, Michael Jr., my team, and Gateway Church. Whether you knew it or not, you have been my ear and support structure, and you have each had a deep effect on my life's story.

ABOUT THE AUTHOR

Matt Knisely is an Emmy Award–winning photojournalist, storyteller, creative director, and artist who loves telling stories of the extraordinary in the ordinary. He serves as the creative director for Gateway Church in Southlake, Texas. Matt is cofounder of Good World Creative, a creative cooperative focused on meaningful visual storytelling to help nonprofits tell their story and enhance their brand. Additionally, he consults with some of today's leading churches, helping them reenvision the power of story and the creative process. He has been described by The National Press Photographers Association as "one of the most versatile photojournalists working today," and he has a national reputation for his unique and teachable approach to TV photojournalism and visual storytelling. Matt's work has won many honors, including Associated Press Southwest

Press Photographer of the Year, twenty Emmy Awards, two prestigious Edward R. Murrow Awards, and more than seventy other regional and national awards. He can be reached at @mattknisely on Twitter or by visiting mattknisely.com.